*Un*Common Sense
...*Apparently!*
"A CALL TO ARMS"

What Has Happened to America...and What We Must Do to Fix It!

T. M. Ballantyne, Jr.

*Un*Common Sense
...Apparently!
"A CALL TO ARMS"

T. M. Ballantyne, Jr.
9 October 2010

First Edition: 1 January 2011

Queen Creek, AZ

Copyright © 2010 by T. M. Ballantyne, Jr.

ISBN-13: 978-0615431932 (Ballantyne Books)

All rights reserved. No part of this book may be reproduced or transmitted in any form or by any means, electronic or mechanical, including photocopying, recording, or by any information storage and retrieval system, without permission in writing from the copyright owner.

This book was printed in the United States of America.

"Next to the gift of life, the right to direct that life is God's greatest gift to man!"

David O. McKay

*Un*Common Sense
...Apparently!
"A CALL TO ARMS"

Table of Contents

Cover Story..I

About the Title..III

Author's Note...V

Preface..IX

Chapter One......**"Choice Architecture"**.........1

Chapter Two.......... **The Constitution and
                       The Rule of Law**..............9

Chapter Three...... **The "*Ism's*"**.....................15

Chapter Four........**The Media
                      "Scoreboard"**...................21

Chapter Five......... **The *Real* "Tea Party"**.....25

Chapter Six...........**The Lens of *Truth***...........33

Chapter Seven.....**The Legal Limits
                     of *Government!***............39

Chapter Eight.......**The Classless Instigators
                      of Class Warfare**...........45

Chapter Nine........***Standing* for Truth - *Ignoring* .Obfuscation**...51

Chapter Ten..........**The Origin of Our Rights and the solution to our problems!**......................55

Chapter Eleven.....**Political Parties and the Debt**......................63

Chapter Twelve.....**The "Plenary Power" To Tax**..............................71

Chapter Thirteen **"All You Need to Know"**...........................75

Chapter Fourteen **Conventional "Wisdom"**..........................83

Chapter Fifteen.....**The *Call to Arms!***..............89

Final Note from the Author.......................101

Appendix I..............**"Quote of the Decade:"**...........................103

Appendix II.......... **A Letter to the President**........................105

About the Author..111

Author's Photo...113

Cover Story

On the 28th of August, 2010, some five weeks prior to the time of this writing, hundreds of thousands of the *"soul of America"* gathered on the Washington Mall, in front of the Lincoln Memorial, to participate in the "Restoring Honor" rally organized and presented by radio/*tv* talk-show host, Glenn Beck.

Wanting to be a part of this national gathering, of those committed to restoring the country to the principles that had made it great, I was fortunate enough to be able to attend the rally, accompanied by a son-in-law and two of my grandsons.

The cover photo was taken by my son-in-law, and shows his oldest son up in one of the trees lining the mall, observing the rally from his exalted vantage point. Unlike most adults, my grandson can see things through "unblemished" eyes – *"above the fray,"* so to speak. He has no "agenda" *or party affiliation!* He also represents our nation's future!

It is my hope that both he and his younger brother will remember the weekend on which they went to our nation's capitol to stand with their father and grandfather, to celebrate our nation's greatness, and restore its timeless values. We concluded our time there by visiting Arlington National Cemetery. It is indeed hallowed ground, and my younger grandson especially seemed to sense its sacred nature.

One key message during the rally that morning, was that *"One person can change the world!"* and *"That one person is you!"* And so Glenn challenged each of us, to *"do our part"* to restore our nation to its original stature, *as a beacon of freedom and prosperity* - or words to that effect. He further challenged us to find out what *we individually* could do to make a difference. So I accepted his challenge, and some six weeks later had "found my voice" in the process of writing this book. *Doing so has galvanized my own resolve!*

I therefore dedicate this book to all those who gathered on the Mall on the 28th of August, 2010, to stand up for America...*and to all those who gathered at the polls*, on November 2nd, to *begin* the process of restoring our country, and our way of life. May God bless us in our determination to do so...and *may God bless America!*

Cover Design by Jodee Ballantyne – *ThePhotographingEdge.com*

About the Title

It must be apparent to anyone versed in the lore of the first *American Revolution* that my title was taken from the most influential political tract in our nation's history – and, no doubt, *the most important pamphlet in all of history – Common Sense,* by Thomas Paine. It was also, of course, borrowed and used most recently as the title of the *New York Time's #1 Best Seller*, by my (and America's) good friend, Glenn Beck. So why *Un*Common Sense?

Well, I first meant it to reflect the fact that what was once *common sense*, and *obvious* to virtually *everyone*, has become entirely *un*-common today – at least in the *public* discourse. The principles upon which this nation was founded, however, remain both *common sense* and obvious to the vast majority of hard-working Americans today!

I'm talking about the bedrock principles of individual liberty – the right to govern our own lives – hard work, and self-determination – the freedom to decide who and what we will be, without any*thing* or any*body* telling us that we can't – and personal accountability. These are the principles and values that made this the once freest and most prosperous nation ever to be found on Earth!

While working with my daughter Jodee, a photographer and graphic designer, on the book's cover, I learned that she assumed that the term (*un*common) referred to the fact that what passes today as reason or intelligence among the ruling elites is, in fact, *un*-common sense – *if it can be called "sense" at all.*

The sad thing, of course (and this is what a good part of this book is about) is that the "discourse" of the elites – from the lecture halls and classrooms of college campuses nationwide, to virtually every local and national radio and *TV* "news" cast and "news" paper in the country – defines the discourse of the general populace...and it is indeed *un* – common sense!

Fortunately, WE THE PEOPLE still know better, and it is with our own common sense that we will once more save this nation! It is my sincere hope that the *common sense facts and solutions* outlined herein *will arm us for the battle that lies ahead….*

Author's Note

So who am I, and what are my qualifications to address *you*, my fellow citizens? My qualifications are, in fact, only one: I am nothing more, nor less, than one of THE PEOPLE of this great nation. I hold no office – other than those of husband, father, grandfather – nor do I hold any advanced academic degrees. I am simply an Architect/Master Builder, and author of several books.

However, I do hold – and share with you – the only legitimate power upon which this (or any other) nation, and its government, can ever rest: *the power represented by the will of THE PEOPLE.* And who was Thomas Paine before *he* wrote *Common Sense?* Just a common citizen who published his thoughts….

It will remain for you, as an individual, and as a citizen, to determine whether or not I have spoken here for you and what you hold dear. I believe I do. It will not be necessary, however, that you or I *convince* any of those who disagree with us.

Those who have "ears to hear" and "eyes to see" will – *as they always have* – recognize and embrace the truth. *Those who have an agenda, or whose party affiliation trumps both truth and reason, will not.* Those who, because of pride, cannot bring themselves to acknowledge that they have been misled, will not. There are, sadly, always those who can behold the sun at noonday, and deny that they are seeing it. In the end, they deceive – and punish – *only themselves*….These are they for whom we have been admonished to pray – *and we shall*.

We, meanwhile, who have embraced the truth of the inspired system of government created by our founders, can find great joy in sharing our understanding with others. *Let us, therefore, "be about [our] Father's business"!*

"They [the principles of freedom (contained in the Constitution)] should be the creed of our political faith – the text of civil instruction – the touchstone by which to try the service of those we trust [to represent us]; and should we wander from them in moments of error or alarm, let us hasten to retrace our steps and to regain the road which alone leads to peace, liberty, and safety."

Thomas Jefferson – from his *First Inaugural Address, March 4, 1801*

www.nccs.net/articles/ril71.html

VI

"The principles of Jefferson are the definitions and axioms of free society. And yet they are denied, and evaded, with no small [degree] of success….But soberly, it is now no child's play to save the principles of Jefferson from total overthrow in this nation."

Abraham Lincoln – *Letter to Henry L. Pierce and others* – *April 6, 1859* – *Collected Works 3:375*

http://showcase.netins.net/web/creative/lincoln/speeches/pierce.htm

Preface

It is with both focused determination and supreme confidence that I address those among us that still cherish freedom...*as we live in a day when the timeless principles upon which this nation was founded are under assault.* There are among us those who, by their own admission, use or *create* either real or perceived circumstances, in order to facilitate further government intrusion into our laws and our lives. For now, they have succeeded at both finding and creating the crises they have needed and *sought*, in order to carry out their camouflaged designs. Now we, as a nation, and as a people, are stepping forward *to deny them* the misfortune of "fundamentally transforming" the greatest nation on Earth...*and we will succeed!*

In reality, we have been doing so since the beginning of this most recent onslaught against our freedoms and our sovereign will as a people. Our country and its constitution have been steadily eroded, both prior to and throughout our lifetimes, but we once again find ourselves on the brink of total abandonment of the principles and ideals announced to the world in both the *Constitution* and the *Declaration of Independence*.

While the once "mainstream" media – now, at the very least, *collusive* with our *unconstitutional* and, therefore, *unlawful* government – disparage the true mainstream of this great nation (the *912-ers,* the *Tea Party,* the *everyday citizens* throughout the country running for state and national office), and trumpets the message that amidst a nearly 10% *reported* unemployment we are in "Recovery Summer," not only is our economy far worse than at any previous period in our lifetimes, but every step the government has taken – *and continues to take* – could *only* be calculated to further cripple us or bring us to our knees!

"Society in every state is a blessing, but government even in its best state is but a necessary evil; in its worst state an intolerable one."

               Thomas Paine – *Common Sense*

"The greatest [calamity] which could befall [us would be] submission to a government of unlimited powers."

    Thomas Jefferson – *Declaration and Protest of Virginia, 1825*
        http://etext.virginia.edu/jefferson/quotations/jeff1060.htm

The good news, however, is that *we as a people have awakened!* We have seen and – more importantly – *felt* the effects of a state-controlled economy, buttressed by an apparently state-controlled establishment media, while an unconstitutional system of unelected, and unaccountable Czars (expanded under the previous Administration) with radical resumes and agenda, seeks to control virtually every aspect of our lives with wanton disregard, even disdain, for the *Constitution* and our *unalienable rights*...and *we are outraged by it!*

While our country as a whole began to pull away sharply from its constitutional moorings nearly a hundred years ago, under President Woodrow Wilson – with the introduction of the "progressive" income tax and the establishment of the Federal Reserve – after the Great Depression and World War II our hope in general, and faith in our systems of government and free-enterprise, were so renewed that as a nation we once again began to prosper exceedingly.

Unfortunately we prospered to such a degree that as a nation we began to focus solely on creating wealth, and indulging ourselves in the fruits thereof. This resulted in the false security that our government and our elected leaders would always do what was in our best interest. Under this delusion we continued to focus on work and wealth, and we failed to watch what was going on, or to hold our elected officials accountable, as our government grew wildly, spilling far beyond its constitutional bounds; growing from expenditures of $35 Billion in 1947 to $3.5 Trillion last year (2009) – *a growth of 100 times its size in just over 60 years!* (http://federal-budget.findthebest.com/).

The yearly *deficit* grew from (a surplus) of $4 Billion in 1947, to $3.1 Billion in 1950, to $1.6 Trillion this year – a growth of 500+ times in 60 years!

During roughly that same time period, the US population grew from 150,697,361 in 1950*, to 310,406,312 today,** approximately doubling, *while yearly government spending increased a hundredfold, and yearly deficit spending increased over five-hundredfold!*

* http://www.factmonster.com/ us/census/national-1790-2000.html

** http://www.census.gov/main/www/popclock.html

Now that we are awake, we must arrest the rising tide that threatens to sweep away all that we hold dear. Now is the time, *and I have every confidence that we will succeed in this hour of our country's greatest need!*

For those who love "the world," and the "praise of men," more than they love the truth, and the Author of all truth, all that they are left with is the "foolishness of men." Built upon a foundation of falsehoods, they can only arrive at, frankly, *comical* (yet *absurd*) conclusions. Thus a "celebrity," or public figure, can exult in *the philosophy of Mao* (Former White House Communications Director, Anita Dunn – http://www.youtube.com/watch?v=Fi1zg2NOCn8), or the genius of *Fidel*:

> "Meeting Fidel Castro were (sic) the eight most important hours of my life."
> Steven Spielberg

> "*Viva Fidel! Viva Che [Guevarra]!* Castro is the most honest and courageous politician I've ever met."
> Jesse Jackson

> "Very selfless and moral. One of the world's wisest men."
> Oliver Stone

> "*Cuba's Elvis.*"
> Dan Rather

> "A Dream come true." [*Who's* dream?]
> Supermodel Naomi Campbell

"Socialism works. I think Cuba can prove that."

Chevy Chase

"Castro is an extraordinary man. He is warm and understanding and seems extremely humane."

Gina Lollobrigida

http://archive.newsmax.com/archives/articles/2005/3/29/151036.shtml

Both Mao and Fidel were responsible for not only enslaving, but for *killing* thousands of people (millions in the case of Mao), along with another Hollywood favorite, "Che" (Guevarra), and yet they are all but worshipped by the Left. While the "progressives" feign shock and dismay when the politicians and policies they support and promote are even *insinuated* to be "socialist," *they – unlike the vast majority of Americans –* clearly embrace the demonstrably false assertion that "*Socialism works*"...for the masses, at least!

This is who and what we are up against – all denials by themselves (and those among them who occupy the media spotlight) to the contrary. They in no way represent the heart and soul of America, and *their vision for a 'fundamentally transformed' "America" will not stand!* However,

We are not finished! In fact, *"[We] have [just] begun to fight!"*

John Paul Jones - 23 September 1779 (adapted)

http://teaparty07.wordpress.com/2008/01/11/i-have-not-yet-begun-to-fight-john-paul-jones/

*Un*Common Sense
...*Apparently!*

"A CALL TO ARMS"

Chapter One

"Choice Architecture"

"Four score and seven years ago our fathers brought forth on this continent, a new nation, conceived in Liberty, and dedicated to the proposition that all men are created equal.

Now we are engaged in a great civil war, testing whether that nation, or any nation so conceived and so dedicated, can long endure."

Abraham Lincoln - Gettysburg Address

The conflict in which we are now engaged is itself a civil war – albeit a war of words or ideas (*not unlike the first American Revolution*) – in which the nature and the future of our nation will be determined; and, make no mistake, *it is a war for the souls of men,* also dedicated by those on the side of THE PEOPLE *"to the proposition that all men are created equal."*

We are now engaged in a Second great American Revolution! And while it was perfectly understood by both our Founders and the people of this nation throughout most of its relatively short history, that the phrase *"created equal"* in no way implied (or implies) that the natural gifts and talents of people – and their resulting success or failure – are, or *could* ever be, equal, there are those today who *purport* that their interest is in making the *results* of all people equal. (Some, of course – *particularly the ruling elites* – will be *"more equal than others!"* George Orwell, *1984*).

"The dream wasn't to have a black man in the White House. It was to have everything equal in everybody's house."

Congressman Al Sharpton – from his own 8/28 (2010) *Martin Luther King Rally*

Let it be clearly understood that the idea of everyone being equal, or having exactly the same result – regardless of individual efforts or abilities – is entirely incompatible with the very premise of freedom. Inherent in – and central to – the concept of individual liberty is the principle of personal responsibility. How free is one to choose if he is shielded from the consequences of his choices?

The only way to remove the danger or the possibility of falling – the *freedom* to fall, actually! – is to take away the freedom to climb, or the freedom to fly! It is *law,* and it can and will *never be otherwise!*

We, of course, live in a day in which the government has taken it upon itself to decide who fails and who doesn't. Sounds great, right? Do not be so naïve as to think that once this happens, that same government will not, in the next breath, also restrict the choices of those they now presume to "parent," and "protect." What they are really doing is *encouraging* the very recklessness (freedom from accountability!) that led to the crisis in the first place.

While this has traditionally been called "regulation," it is now being *effervescently hailed* as "choice architecture," by those who seek what is "best" for us (*Nudge: Improving Decisions about Health, Wealth, and Happiness,* by Richard H. Thaler and Cass R. Sunstein).

They acknowledge that there are those (with common, or *un*common sense, *apparently!*) who fear that this could lead to *"Big Brother."* This they dismiss; adding, however, that as long as *someone* has to make the decision regarding where to put the "salad bar" relative to the "burgers," *"why not do it in such a way as to make people healthier and happier?"*

What they leave out, of course, is *who gets to make those initial choice*s – in order to "nudge" the unthinking and incapable masses into making the "right" choice. The idea that it could or should be the cafeteria *owner* is, of course, unthinkable in *Utopia.* What if he or she doesn't know what is "best"? Well, *we can't afford to take that chance!*

Re-enter Cass Sunstein – this time as the "Information and Regulatory Czar," or head of the *Office of Information and Regulatory Affairs,* working in the White House, being handsomely compensated, while deciding which choices the "Homer Simpsons" of the world (http://politifi.com/ news/Cass-Sunstein-Americans-Are-Like-Homer-Simpson-too-stupid-to-get-it-1155034.html) will be *allowed* to make. Actually (*initially,* at least), we will still get to make *all* of the ultimate choices...from among the *cafeteria options* which Cass and his staff decide we should be offered.

Are you getting this? Are you outraged yet? I think you are!

In a January 11, 2009 article on the *Constitutional Law Prof Blog* (http://lawprofessors.typepad.com/conlaw/2009/01/cass-sunstein-p.html), entitled *Cass Sunstein Post in Obama Administration*, we read the following:

"Sunstein brings a measure of star power to the post, as a leading constitutional scholar and the Felix Frankfurter professor of law at Harvard. He joined the Harvard faculty this year after many years at the University of Chicago, where he is still a visiting professor. He and Obama taught there."

Clearly, he's no *Homer Simpson*, but he does sound like someone whom we can trust…*doesn't he?* There's more to the article however:

"It's worth remembering that Sunstein has recently achieved great fame for Nudge, a book which basically argues that we need to apply the insights of behavioral economics to the construction of regulation. And Director of the Office of Information and Regulatory Affairs is the ultimate staging ground for those ideas. Reagan understood that OIRA was the central clearinghouse where you could affect the whole of the regulatory state all at once. He wanted to virtually shut it down."

I will conclude this note on freedom, by pointing out that those on the Left see nothing wrong – either morally or philosophically – with the idea of a federal government and bureaucracy so broad and powerful that it even presumes to tell its citizens which foods they should and shouldn't eat.

Now I ask you, is this *your* world view, or is it the world view of anyone you know or associate with? Is it, or was it, the world view of *any* of our founders or other great leaders? *Washington? Jefferson? Franklin? John or Samuel Adams? Patrick Henry? Abraham Lincoln?* Is this the philosophy that you grew up with, or that *you believe* made America great?

And finally, *do you really think that this is what most Americans believe in their hearts?* I think we all know the answer to that…and yet, those in control of our country today, as well as our universities, and the "traditional" media *do* believe it, and they want you to think that "everyone else" believes it as well!

For those who naively believe that this is an exaggeration, I will point to two very timely examples. The first came out of the recent Senate confirmation hearings for Supreme Court nominee Elana Kagan. When pressed to answer whether, in her opinion, the federal government had the authority to restrict the food that people eat, she could not – or *would not* – give a simple or direct answer.

For the second example, witness the current First Lady's "anti-obesity campaign," and hear what she has to say about *"choices."* By the way, is *fighting obesity* a good thing? Most would agree that it is. Is it the role of the federal government to do so? If it is, in fact, a noble cause, *why shouldn't it be?*

I suggest that the question regarding its nobility is irrelevant. From the perspective of the law, there is only one question that need be asked: Does the *Constitution of the United States* grant to the Congress the power to regulate the citizens' diets? Before answering, however, ask yourself this: Can you imagine John Adams (the "father" of the *Declaration of Independence*), Thomas Jefferson (the *writer* of the *Declaration*), or James Madison (the father of the *Constitution*) answering *"Yes"?*

If you have read anything that the founders had to say about the limited federal government they were seeking to establish, you realize the absurdity of the question itself. Their response, were it asked, however, would be an astonished incredulity on their part, followed by a resounding *"No!"*

Meanwhile, this is what the First Lady had to say about diets (*not* about the *Constitution!*):

"That's why I want to challenge every restaurant to offer healthy menu options and then provide them up front so that parents don't have to hunt around and read the small print to find an appropriately sized portion [!] that doesn't contain levels -- high levels of fat, salt and sugar".

"No man [or woman] is good enough to govern another man without that other's consent."

Abraham Lincoln – Speech at Peoria, Illinois - October 16, 1854
Collected Works of Abraham Lincoln. Volume 2

Do you really want the government, whose primary responsibilities are to defend your freedoms and protect you from unwarranted invasion, to tell you what type and what-sized food portions are "appropriate"? How would Patrick Henry have responded to this? Would he have allowed it? Of course he wouldn't...nor will we!

"These choices have to be easy to make and they have to give parents the confidence to know that they can go into any restaurant in this country and choose a genuinely healthy meal for their kids....what it doesn't mean is providing just one token healthy option on the menu...

You could make healthy sides like apple slices or carrots the default choice in a menu and make fries something customers have to request..."

(From the *Future of Capitalism* website: http://www.futureofcapitalism.com/2010/09/michelle-obama-versus-french-fries.)

Suddenly, Marie Antoinette's alleged quip, *"Let them eat cake!"* seems almost *compassionate!* How does one measure the arrogance (or the "audacity") of someone who proposes to dictate to a free man or a free woman what he or she should eat?

This attempt is nothing particularly new, however, as the federal government has – at no small expense to us, the taxpayers – for years waged a war on salt. More recently, however, the "Republican" Mayor of New York City has taken it upon himself to save the inhabitants of the *Big Apple* from this deadly poison (without which the human species could not survive!). Apparently, there were already restrictions on *trans fats* in place. What is next? (The answer, of course, is *sugar,* and already *"Coke"* machines are being banned on school campuses in a number of locations...but I digress!) In a January 11, 2010 article on the *reason.com* website, entitled "The Shaky Science Underlying New York's Salt Assault," by Jacob Sullum, we read that:

"Participation in New York City's new anti-salt campaign, which aims to reduce the sodium content of restaurant and packaged food by an average of 25 percent in the next five years, is voluntary for now. But that is also how the city's trans fat ban got started; when restaurants declined to cooperate, they were forced. City officials are downplaying the possibility that recalcitrant volunteers will be conscripted. "There's not an easy regulatory fix," Associate Health Commissioner Geoffrey Cowley told The New York Times. "You would have to micromanage so many targets for so many different products" (http://reason.com/blog/2010/01/11/the-shaky-science-underlying-n).

Really? Think how efficiently this could – and *would* – be managed by the federal government under nationalized "health care" – if it were not reversed. (For the record, *I have complete confidence that it will be!*) New York City's population is just over 8 million (8,008,278), while that of the entire US is roughly 310 million – that's nearly 40 times (38+) larger, and United States Department of Health and Human Services-Secretary Kathleen Sebelius *would be* regulating far more than sodium, trans fat, and sugar!

(www.citypopulation.de/USA-NewYorkCity.html).

While the government's accounting practices (defined by Congress) *allow (!)* the Congress to *underreport* the real debt, the unfunded liabilities of Social Security and Medicare (which, while being by far the *largest* liabilities, are somehow *not required to be reported!*) may now be approaching $200,000,000,000,000 – that's $200 Trillion! (http://www.minyanville.com/assets/File/Kotlikoff_USBankruptcy_paper%5B1%5D.pdf) – and they are vastly simpler to manage than one sixth of the entire US economy, and, incidentally, *the health care needs of every man, woman, and child in America!* Could any sane person *actually believe* that this is doable...*by government bureaucrats,* no less?

In addition, could any *honest person* suggest with a straight face that we will soon be providing free health care for an additional 50,000,000 (50 million) people, and that our individual health care costs – including the dramatically increased taxes (which, of course, are never mentioned – *or factored in*, no doubt) – are going to go down? Of course not, *but all they needed to do was get something in place*....

Already, since the passage of the bill, health care premiums have increased significantly for some, *dramatically* for others, partly in order for insurance companies to cushion themselves against the reduced profits that are inevitable (or would be if the bill were not repealed). If one's ultimate goal, however, is a single-payer system, as the President (http://www.youtube.com/watch?v=fpAyan1fXCE&feature=related) and other Congressional leaders have openly admitted, then the rising insurance premiums are the perfect (i.e., intentional) way of *forcing* the people to beg for a solution – which, of course, the government is ready (and *waiting!*) to supply.

Meanwhile, how is it that almost no politician in the country who voted for this massive take-over ran on that record in 2010, while many, *even those whose party forced it through against the will of a sizable majority of the American people* (54% Opposed – 41% In Favor, according to at least one national poll)

(**http:**//www.rasmussenreports.com/public_content/politics/current_events/healthcare/september_2009/health_care_reform),

are running on the fact that they voted *against* it? What more need be said? (See Chapter Thirteen: *"All You Need to Know."*)

And yet the president, the congressional leaders, and the elite media want you to believe that this is both wonderful and wildly popular. (It is so popular that the president is now soliciting church leaders to tell their parishioners how compassionate the entire thing is!)

If one doubts that this is *not doable* or possible – even if it were desirable, or *legal* under the *Constitution* – he need look no further than Canada or Great Britain, or all of Europe, with populations vastly smaller than our own, to see that this utopian idea is pure fantasy. It hasn't worked anywhere that it has been tried, on a large scale.

While Denmark is alleged by some to provide a successful model, the population of Denmark was only 5,493,621 in 2008, and is expected to fall. That makes it 1.77% of the US population – less than 2% - and only two thirds the size of New York City.

Chapter Two

The Constitution and the Rule of Law

It should be noted that Cass Sunstein apparently finds the *Constitution*, *as it was written*, to be fairly irrelevant to our 'Brave New World.'

"Some conservative legal thinkers like Justice Scalia, Justice Thomas think that the Constitution means what it originally meant [!]. That means we should understand the document by going into a kind of 'time machine' and capturing the public understanding of the public that ratified the document a century or more than a century ago."

http://notalemming.wordpress.com/2010/09/26/cass-sunstein-most-conservatives-view-of-the-constitution-requires-a-time-machine/

Earth to our "Information" (and Regulatory) Czar: The *Internet* (invented by someone who shares your view of the *Constitution*) makes it possible to read the actual words of the "public" that wrote "the document." Since you, Cass, no doubt believe, that the "General Welfare" clause allows, or authorizes, you to institute "choice architecture," and "national health care," take over car companies, banks, and now, under "Financial Reform," any business that is "involved in 'finance' " (name one that *isn't!*), here is just a taste of what one can find on the subject with the mere click of a mouse:

"They are not to do anything they please to provide for the general welfare.... [G]iving a distinct and independent power to do any act they please which may be good for the Union, would render all the preceding and subsequent enumerations of power completely useless. It would reduce the whole instrument to a single phrase, that of instituting a Congress with power to do whatever would be for the good of the United States; and as they are the sole judges of the good or evil, it would be also a power to do whatever evil they please."

Thomas Jefferson – *Letter to William Branch Giles, 1825. ME 16:147*

http://etext.virginia.edu/jefferson/quotations/jeff1020.htm

"If Congress can do whatever in their discretion can be done by money, and will promote the General Welfare, the Government is no longer a limited one, possessing enumerated powers, but an indefinite [and unlimited] one...."

James Madison – Letter to Edmund Pendleton, January 21, 1792

Boy, this 'time machine' – called the *Internet* – is "inconvenient!" (How *truly* ironic!) But wait...there's more!

"A wise and frugal government, which shall leave men free to regulate their own pursuits of industry and improvement, and shall not take from the mouth of labor the bread it has earned - this is the sum of good government."

Thomas Jefferson - 1st Inaugural, 1801. ME 3:320

"If we can prevent the government from wasting the labors of the people under the pretense of taking care of them, they must become happy."

Thomas Jefferson – Letter to Thomas Cooper, 1802. ME 10:342

I can only agree with my friend Glenn Beck! *It is as if the founders were writing to us today, rather than to their contemporaries!* It's also as if *they* got into a 'time machine' (*sorry, Cass*) and traveled some 200 years into the future, *and saw exactly what was taking place in our day...and then told us precisely what to do about it!*

And if these gems are of no interest to the *Information* Czar, then perhaps the thoughts of the author of the *Declaration of Independence*, on how the *Constitution* should be interpreted, would interest him. (It will be noted that Mr. Jefferson's position is in *direct opposition* to that of Mr. Sunstein – a "constitutional *scholar*.")

"On every question of construction carry ourselves back [in a 'time machine,' no doubt!] to the time when the Constitution was adopted, recollect the spirit manifested in the debates and instead of trying what meaning may be squeezed out of the text or invented against it, conform to the probable one in which it was passed."

Thomas Jefferson – *Letter to William Johnson, 1823. ME 15:449*

While the following is not a quote from one of our founders (I was unable to discover the name of its author), it is nonetheless so clear in dismissing the notion of the *Constitution* as a "living document" that can or *should* be interpreted in any way that its readers may find convenient, that I include it here:

"The purpose of a written constitution is entirely defeated if, in interpreting it as a legal document, its provisions are manipulated and worked around so that the document means whatever the manipulators wish. Jefferson recognized this danger and spoke out constantly for careful adherence to the Constitution as written, with changes to be made by amendment, not by tortured and twisted interpretations of the text."

http://etext.virginia.edu/jefferson/quotations/jeff1020.htm

While the founders obviously foresaw that circumstances would arise that could require an adaptation of the *Constitution*, and therefore made provisions therein for an amendment process, they were decidedly opposed to this being too easily (and therefore, *too often*) done.

Quoting Thomas Jefferson (from *Wikipedia*):

"I am not an advocate for frequent changes in laws and constitutions, but laws and institutions must go hand in hand with the progress of the human mind. As that becomes more developed, more enlightened, as new discoveries are made, new truths discovered and manners and opinions change, with the change of circumstances, institutions must advance also to keep pace with the times. We might as well require a man to wear still the coat which fitted him when a boy as civilized society to remain ever under the regimen of their barbarous ancestors." [13]

Continuing to quote from *Wikipedia:*

"But he also warned against treating the Constitution as 'a mere thing of wax in the hands of the judiciary, which they may twist, and shape into any form they please.'[14] Jefferson's understanding of how the Constitution should be interpreted is made clear in a letter he wrote March 27, 1801, after assuming the Presidency, 'The Constitution on which our union rests, shall be administered by me according to the safe and honest meaning contemplated by the plain understanding of the people of the United States, at the time of its adoption,—a meaning to be found in the explanations of those who advocated (it)...These explanations are preserved in the publications of the time [(and are easily accessed today via the Internet)], and are too recent in the memories of most men to admit of question.' "

http://en.wikipedia.org/wiki/Living_Constitution

If the Constitutional views of our now-favorite Czar (Of course we love them all – *all 38 of them?*) are not enough to reassure you that *he would never overstep his authority* (which apparently has *no basis in law*), then you should at least know how he views *you*, the typical American, and what he can do for (or *to*) you:

"Once we know that people are human, and have some Homer Simpson in them, then there is a lot that can be done to manipulate them."
http://www.foxnews.com/story/0,2933,601362,00.html

If all of this isn't bad enough, what is actually worse is the fact that the elitist media will not – *has* not – reported any of it; only the *new media* – *Fox News* (esp. Glenn Beck), *Talk Radio*, and the *Internet/Blogosphere*. (In spite of the President promising a new "transparency" in the government, his Information Czar – appointed "temporarily" *without the approval of Congress* – has not spoken to the public, nor to the Congress, granted any interviews, nor answered any questions from reporters [which, if of any consequence, would *only come* from *new media* entities]).

So, we have come to a point in our history where we must make a choice between *deciding for ourselves,* and having an *Information and Regulatory Czar (with a necessarily endless staff over time)* decide which "choice *options*" are available to all of us – for the purpose of "Improving Decisions about [*our?*] Health, Wealth, and Happiness."

The wonderful thing, of course, is that should we show a tendency to choose "incorrectly," we will be "nudged" (initially) towards making the "correct" choice. In the end, we *will (vil?),* of course, make the right one! Even more wonderful is the assurance that when all is said and done, *we will all be "equal" in every way!* As pointed out, however, *"Some will [still!] be 'more equal' than others!"*

Chapter Three

The "*Ism's*"

If you've seen one, you've seen 'em all'!

None of this is new, of course. It was formalized by Karl Marx and Frederick Engels, a century and a half ago, and subsequently tried in the former Soviet Union, under Vladimir Lenin and Joseph Stalin; in Nazi Germany (the National *Socialist* Party), under Adolf Hitler; in Italy (the Italian *Social* Republic), under Tito Mussolini; in the People's Republic of China, under Mao Tse-Tung; by the Cambodian Communists (the Khmer Rouge, in Democratic Kampuchea), under Pol Pot; by the Cubans, under Fidel Castro; advocated by the Black Panthers ("Ideology: Marxism-Leninism, Maoism, internationalism, black nationalism, socialism" – from *Wikipedia*), in our own country during the late 1960's and into the mid 1970's; and by today's North Korean and Chinese Governments – to name some of the "grander" experiments.

Those on the Left will, of course, immediately cry *"Foul!"* claiming that these are all communist or "fascist" countries or dictators, and that they, the "Progressives" or American Left, only espouse the rights of "workers," or the "poor," or other *"disenfranchised"* minorities. They will further – for national consumption, at least – claim that they are not even "socialist!" This, of course, is ludicrous, as some within the ranks of the current administration have openly acknowledged their affiliation to revolutionary communism (Van Jones) and its leaders (Anita Dunn), while others (Donald Berwick) have openly and forcefully advocated Marxist doctrines such as the redistribution of wealth.

Here is just a taste of this *view* and the way the current Administration has "taken questions" regarding its proponent. It will be noted that this is a textbook example of how the Left cannot (for fear of backlash from "common" or *"average"* people) and will not be open or honest about their true positions and intentions.

This is also *conclusive proof* of the fact that they *know* – in spite of the consistent media chorus to the contrary, and all of the liberal politicians' claims that *"the 'American people' want this,"* or, *"the 'American people' don't want that"* – that mainstream Americans do not buy *the rhetoric of redistribution!*

In spite of years of media pounding on the "self-evident" *selfishness* of "big business" or "Capitalism" in general (subtle, or *"subliminal,"* for the most part), we, THE PEOPLE, still believe that this is the greatest nation on earth, and *"the land of opportunity," and countless other such 'old fashioned' ideas.* Apparently, *we just don't get it!* We just need to be "nudged" a little...or, perhaps, *a lot!*

And now for the "evidence" –

(CNSNews.com) – "Donald Berwick, an advocate of health care rationing and redistributing wealth through the health-care system, who President Barack Obama appointed administrator of the Centers for Medicare and Medicaid Services (CMS) without a Senate confirmation hearing or vote, will not answer questions from the U.S. Senate, according to members of the committee that has oversight over his nomination.

" 'We've been trying to get him to answer questions in writing. He won't do that,' Sen. Orrin Hatch (R-Utah), a member of the Senate Finance Committee, told CNSNews.com Thursday. 'We've been trying to get him up for a hearing. He won't do that. He has indicated he might come to a hearing. So far, it's been unsuccessful, no matter how important these matters are.' "

http://www.cnsnews.com/news/article/75734

With regard to my list of radical (Communist and Fascist) Leftists, *today's* Left will also hasten to add that both Hitler and Mussolini were, in "fact," on the *"Right"* – *even* the "Christian Right" in the case of the Nazi dictator. The latter assertions, while both meaningless and absurd, have long since been considered – and routinely reported – as "settled science," by those by the Left!

As previously indicated, Hitler's party was the *National Socialist Party*, but both Hitler and his Italian ally, Mussolini, are considered "fascists." Mussolini is the father of "fascism," a totalitarian form of government, which while it opposed (Soviet) communism, is the antithesis of libertarianism and free-market capitalism.

Quoting once more from *Wikipedia*, as it describes the *fascists:* *"They claim that culture is created by the collective national society and its state, that cultural ideas are what give individuals identity, and thus they reject individualism. Viewing the nation as an integrated collective community, they see pluralism as a dysfunctional aspect of society, and justify a totalitarian state as a means to represent the nation in its entirety."*

One may quibble over "what the definition of *is* is," but the above is textbook collectivism (statism, socialism, communism, et al.), and the polar opposite of the individual liberty and economic freedom espoused by the conservative "Right." And while those wedded to the victimhood philosophy of the Left, may never acknowledge the truth of this one simple fact, any honest – and rational – observer can see that it is so. Thus, there is no need to engage in debate over claims that conservatives are "fascists." Fascism is – *in principle as well as in practice* – a wholly-owned subsidiary of the Left!

The supposed basis of this assertion is that those of us on the Right would force our (Christian) values on others. While I, for one, openly avow that it is the right and duty of society to preserve long-standing moral standards for the preservation of society as a whole (such as those given by our Creator in the *Ten Commandments*), we have never in our history as a nation forced individuals to adopt a specified set of values or beliefs; nor will conservatives do so in the future.

To pretend, however, that subjecting members of society to "sensitivity training," or trying persons for "hate crimes" on the basis of alleged feelings or thoughts (proven or otherwise), is anything short of forcibly imposing a set of values, one must, of necessity, be either naïve or dishonest – even if their true purpose is to achieve some "noble" political end...such as exclusive (superior, in fact, as well as *unconstitutional*) status for his or her own favored group.

Furthermore, is not forcing one to use only a certain type of light bulb, or purchase a specified health-insurance (or, for that matter, retirement-) policy, or ingest no more than a certain amount of salt, or leave no more than a federally allowable "carbon footprint," the height of fascist imposition or control?

Yes, we too are once again engaged in an historic conflict to determine whether a *"nation, conceived in Liberty, and dedicated to the proposition that all men are created equal...can [or will] endure." I, for one, have no doubt that it will, but it is time for us to stop the mad rush to total state control of our country and of our lives!*

All that we must do is follow what we know in our hearts to be true – that this nation, founded on the principles of individual liberty and personal initiative (within our system of free enterprise), became the greatest and most prosperous nation to ever grace the planet...while all others, not so conceived, *have not endured!* We must look to ourselves, and be guided in our *actions* (such as determining how we will vote) by our own convictions, *and not look to the elites in both media and government who purport to speak for the majority.*

They speak only for themselves, and for *what they want us to believe* are the views of our fellow Americans. *They are not*, and we will no longer submit to this or any other *"form of tyranny over the mind of man"* (Thomas Jefferson – *in a letter to Benjamin Rush, Sep 23, 1800 –*
http://wiki.answers.com/Q/Thomas_Jefferson_wrote_I_have_sworn_upon_the_altar_of_God_eternal_hostility_against_every_form_of_tyranny_over_the_mind_of_man._What_does_it_mean*).*

Because the truth is now available to us through a myriad of means and sources, we can no longer be 'lead to the slaughter!' As Americans, we value our independence and our God-given right to pursue our dreams; and we reject the false assertion that it is the role of government at *any* level to take care of us! That is as preposterous as it is unworkable, not to mention being entirely outside of the authority that we, the people, have granted to the government through either the *Declaration* or the *Constitution; and we will not sell our birthright of freedom for a "mess of pottage!"*

"A popular Government without popular information, or the means of acquiring it, is but a Prologue to a Farce or a Tragedy, or perhaps both. Knowledge will forever govern ignorance: And a people who mean to be their own Governors, must arm themselves with the power which knowledge gives."

James Madison - *Letter to W.T. Barry, August 4, 1822*

http://press-pubs.uchicago.edu/founders/documents/v1ch18s35.html

There comes a time when we must hold the facts up to the light of truth. We have a government that was created from an inspired *Constitution* which at once delineates and proscribes its duties and its authority. We also have complete access to the writings of those who conceived and crafted the *Constitution*, and their intentions are readily apparent. So there is no need to conjecture or debate endlessly what they have thoroughly explained and made abundantly clear.

In the coming chapters we will examine what key figures among the founders had to say about the proper role of the federal government (as well as governments in general), and the limits of its authority. It is my position that when the authors of the *Constitution* have been completely clear with regard to the meaning of key provisions in the founding document, the only legal or lawful way in which we can vary from that which they intended is through the officially designated process of amending the document. Short of that, *as the supreme law of the land, it must be followed.*

"Whensoever the General [(Federal)] Government assumes undelegated powers, its acts are unauthoritative, void, and of no force."

Thomas Jefferson – *Draft Kentucky Resolutions, 1798. The Writings of Thomas Jefferson*, (Memorial Edition) Lipscomb and Bergh, editors, ME 17:380

http://press-pubs.uchicago.edu/founders/documents/v1ch8s41.html

"The greatest [calamity] which could befall [us would be] submission to a government of unlimited powers."

Thomas Jefferson – *Declaration and Protest of Virginia, 1825. The Writings of Thomas Jefferson*, (Memorial Edition) Lipscomb and Bergh, editors, ME 17:445

http://etext.virginia.edu/jefferson/quotations/jeff1060.htm

"I consider the foundation of the Constitution as laid on this ground that 'all powers not delegated to the United States, by the Constitution, nor prohibited by it to the states, are reserved to the states or to the people.' To take a single step beyond the boundaries thus specially drawn around the powers of Congress, is to take possession of a boundless field of power not longer susceptible of any definition."

Thomas Jefferson – *Letter to George Washington, Opinion on the Constitutionality of a National Bank, February 15, 1791*

http://www.consource.org/index.asp?bid=582&documentid=58942

Chapter Four

The Media "Scoreboard"

Fortunately, those of us who share these core American values – and that is *exactly* what they are – make up *the vast majority* of the American public. We have never been the fringe, but until the age of the *new media* our only means of feedback on a broad or national scale was the elite media; and we had no way of disproving what didn't seem to fit with our own observations or reality. We knew almost no one who believed as the media reported, but they remained the sole means of verification outside of our own limited circles, or *spheres,* of influence.

Some years back, I was in an eastern town, on business, and picked up a complimentary copy of *USA Today* as I left the motel. The headline read: "President's Approval Rating Up".

I immediately said to myself, "*I can't believe that!*" That was followed instantly by, "*I don't believe that!*" Every day damning new revelations were surfacing, and I simply couldn't imagine any way that the president's approval rating could be up...except for one – conducting the poll in a way (or with a group) that nets the desired result. Would anyone *do* that? (*Have you ever heard a Senator or a President "bend" the truth?*)

It was at that moment that I realized what the *then*-all-powerful media were: *They were the scoreboard for the country*. It didn't matter how many points might be scored by "our side," against the elitist position, the scoreboard always showed "their side" to be *winning*. We knew we were *winning, but the scoreboard, somehow, always told a different story!*

No matter what happened, the *media side* continued to rack up points...and because there was no other national "news" outlet, everyone had to *assume* that what was being reported was simply *"the way it was"* – or, at least, those who were not arming themselves with truth through *other means* (talk radio, i.e., *Rush Limbaugh,* was *beginning* to emerge) had to assume that!

Here is how this worked then, *and still works today*, on those not availing themselves of the *new media*: The always-smiling news anchor, without any thought or challenge on his or her part, dutifully regurgitates the *AP* "wire feed" (apparently a key source for "local" TV and radio stations nationwide) the latest story on *Global Warming* (or was it *"Climate Change"?*). The whole thing was and is an opinion or theory, and yet it was – and, not surprisingly, even after its key proponents were embarrassingly exposed through extensive leaked emails several years ago, still is – reported as "fact." (For an extensive list of links on the subject see: http://www.climate-gate.org/.)

In typical fashion, the elite media did little (if anything) in the way of "investigative reporting" after the emails were leaked, and were "all over" the *Internet.* That was left to the *new media.* If you care to do your own investigating, just type *cbs, nbc, abc, climategate* into the *Google* browser. (I left out *CNN, CNBC,* and *MSNBC,* but you should see them covered there. For an interesting *YouTube* interview on the matter see: http://www.youtube.com/watch?v=9QuCh7pVXvA.)

Getting back to the "scoreboard" analogy...almost without exception every smiling "reporter" or anchor, on nearly every station (or major newspaper), in every city in the country, reports the identical stories – day after day, week after week, year after year...stories on "climate change," the "green economy," the "health-care *crisis,*" etc.

It all, of course, *sounds* wonderful (or terrible!) For those of us in Arizona, our favorite athlete, Steve Nash (someone whom most of us dearly love *on the court!*) comes on the *TV* to talk about "saving the planet" by "going green" – i.e., *using overtly subsidized solar energy.* We – and this includes the growing number who do not watch local news outlets or take a "news" paper, but simply watch *TV* or listen to the radio (even *talk-radio*) – are *inundated* with these messages...and, ultimately, with the values and philosophy that they represent.

So, here's the deal...you, and everyone else in the country, hear all of these things reported as facts that "everyone" knows and accepts (regardless of how absurd they may seem to you – and probably to every other thinking person out there), and yet the natural impression – which we probably *all accept* (to some degree, at least) on a subconscious or subliminal level (if not on a conscious level) – is twofold:

1.) *Everyone* (else) believes that we need to be concerned about, say, our "carbon footprint," and 2.) If we are not *alone* in our skepticism, we are definitely part of a tiny minority. (Note how the media treat the *Tea Party* as the "fringe.")

Anyone who has been to a *Tea Party* "event" knows that this is absurd. These people are as "mainstream" as you can get. Of course there are some "hard-core" people, just as there are in any demographic, but the vast majority are "typical" Americans. Furthermore, the views held by the *Tea Party* are representative of the views of the majority of Americans – whether they've ever been to a Tea Party event or not! All those who *have been* to an event know that those in attendance were neither "extremist" nor violent; and if they were angry, *it is because they don't take kindly to unlawful tyranny!*

There is yet another message underlying these two, and that is that we *should* (if we want to be loved and accepted by everyone else) believe these things. Don't Leonardo DiCaprio, Halle Berry, and Jennifer Aniston all believe in universal health care and global warming? (Of course they do – *along with every other "cool" person on the planet! 'Sup?*)

If you want an unintentionally revealing video representation of everything I have been saying about the ever present media message that "if you want to be *anyone*, you will believe – and *do* – what we're telling you," just go to:
http://www.huffingtonpost.com/2008/10/01/leo-ellen-halle-and-more_n_130999.html.

For further proof that the media-induced mass hypnosis (*mass hysteria?*) pervades the culture, one need look no further than corporate America. There is only once reason that corporate America would tout the "green movement," and that is that *they too have bought the hype that "everyone" is on board!*

It all becomes a self-fulfilling prophecy, of course. When virtually *every* "news" cast and *every* commercial (as well as much of the actual programming, and nearly *all* of the Hollywood elites themselves) tout the "party" line (literally), then what is the "average" person supposed to think? (They're *supposed* to think exactly what the elites in the "ruling class" *tell them to think!*)

Chapter Five

The *Real* "Tea Party"

Well, what *they* (*we*, actually) are *starting* to think – or *realize* – is that *we have been lied to and mislead* by both the media and the politicians (*even those on "our side"*); and now that we realize that the vast majority of our fellow citizens share our same common sense *American* values (*not one of which* is shared by the ruling class), we are now wide awake...*and poised to take our country back!*

So let me make a prediction: [This was written *before* the 2010 midterm election.] The vast majority of the "Tea Party" candidates who have won in the primaries will win in the General Election four weeks from today, 5 October, 2010 (*some by sizeable margins*) – *including in the states of Delaware and Nevada* (*the "conventional wisdom" of the old-guard Republicans notwithstanding!*).

We have a "new breed" running for office. They are called *citizens!* – and they care nothing for parties...only for principles, *and in 4 weeks they and those like them will bring about the biggest shake-up in the make-up of Congress in our nation's history!* THE PEOPLE are going to take back both the House and the Senate, by huge margins. It *will* happen...*and you can write it down!* (While I was *wrong* in the latter assertion, I ascribe that to three things: The failure of certain candidates to be [and run as] true conservatives – Carly Fiorina, in CA; Republicans actually opposing their Primary victors – Lisa Murkowski in Alaska, and the party "leadership" in Delaware; and union tactics/corruption in Nevada.)

Having said that, *this will only be the beginning.* As I have stated, *the vast majority of us care nothing for party loyalty!* Many of us have been "Republican" our entire lives because we *thought* they were for smaller government, etc. We are not in this for "sport," however – unlike the *party loyalists* on *both* sides, who just want to "win," or "beat" the "enemy." The *enemy* is anyone who seeks to remake America by severing it from its Constitutional roots!

To make this into an *"us vs. them – of political parties"* would be both petty and absurd. What we care about is *restoring America to its* Constitutio*nal roots*, i.e., restoring *the Rule of Law*, and replacing those who would *rule* us with those who, as actual *representatives* and *servants of the people*, will re-enshrine the principles of the Declaration: *"life, liberty, and the pursuit of happiness."*

And here's a message to those who would (*do*, actually) call this "extreme" – *These are not mere words or platitudes to us. They are the bedrock principles upon which this nation was founded, and by which it became the freest and most prosperous nation on earth – at any time in man's brief history on the planet; and they are the principles upon which we, THE PEOPLE of the United States, will soon rebuild our nation!*

For those who do not share these values and beliefs, there are numerous options available to you. The nearest is the "island paradise" which so many of you (or, at least, "yours" – see Preface) cherish; but across the Atlantic you will find an entire continent where you can "have it your way!" (We suggest, however, that you avoid Greece, Portugal, Spain, Ireland, et al.)

So, why would I want to be on record making such predictions? Wouldn't it be "safer" to say nothing? Of course it would. Then why am I doing it? I'll tell you why. At the conclusion of this book, I am going to make a number of bold, but specific, recommendations, and the typical response among the timid – *even among those who would be in favor of most, if not all, of them* – will be that *"they could never pass!"* – similar to what the so-called "wise" amongst Republicans (*and even some conservatives*) are saying about the overall election (*"We will likely take back the House, but not necessarily the Senate."*) *and* a number of the individual candidates. (While I was mistaken in some of my predictions, I believe it is precisely because some, perhaps many, Republicans are not, in fact, true conservatives, willing to stand – and *fight* – on principle!)

Apparently, what happened in New Jersey with the governor's race, and in Massachusetts with the Senate race (the "Kennedy" seat) was lost on them…and perhaps they thought Missouri voting to repeal health care by 71-29% was a fluke as well – *not to mention the slew of well entrenched "Republican" incumbents who have been defeated in the primaries by virtually unknown "Tea Party" candidates*.

For the record, we will see the same result everywhere a similar referendum is on the ballot (Arizona, Colorado, Oklahoma). So we are going to win, and after we win, the only way that we will fail to get what the majority of the people want is if we allow ourselves to be *ruled* by those whom we elect to represent our views – *and that is no longer acceptable!* (Note: The *Lame Duck* was a total disgrace!)

The simple fact is that because of a greatly increased access to the truth, an awareness of the radical assault on our nation – on the *Constitution* itself, on our personal freedoms, on the free enterprise system, and on our core American values – *the sleeping giant has been awakened...and yes, we are not happy about it!*

To see our country and our most cherished values under attack and not be unhappy about it would be to allow the elites to control not only our thoughts, but also our feelings and, ultimately, our actions. They love to denounce the "hatred" on our side, but readily dismiss *even the violence* which has been almost exclusively seen on their side. Why should we care what they think? *The simple truth is that we do not*...and, until our "leaders" join us, *they* will continue to be *mislead!*

I am reminded of what the architectural critic for the equivalent of "the newspaper of record" asked the great architect, Howard Roark, in *The Fountainhead,* by libertarian Ayn Rand. *"What do you think of what I have written (about Roark and the other architects of his day)?"* To which Roark replied, *"I don't!"* That is exactly what our attitude towards the elitist media should be! *They do not exist, as far as I am concerned.* While I used to read their papers daily, as well as watch the nightly news, I would no longer even consider reading one, or watching one of their "news" casts. I have no use for disinformation and untruths!

For those who may think this radical, perhaps you would be interested in what Thomas Jefferson, one of our nation's wisest and most learned men, had to say on the subject:

"I do not take a single newspaper, nor read one a month, and I feel myself infinitely the happier for it." - Letter to Tenche Coxe – May 1, 1794

http://oll.libertyfund.org/index.php?option=com_staticxt&staticfile=advanced_search.php

"From forty years' experience of the wretched guess-work of the newspapers...I rarely think them worth reading, and almost never worth notice." Letter to James Monroe, 1816. ME 14:430

"Nothing can now be believed which is seen in a newspaper."
Letter to John Norvell, 1807. ME 11:224
(For *much* more see: http://etext.virginia.edu/jefferson/quotations/jeff1600.htm.)

You may never have been to a *Tea Party* event, locally or nationally, but be assured that their message of a *much* smaller and *less-intrusive* government, lower taxes, and the *freedom* to make of ourselves what we will, is the message that we as a people have believed throughout our history. The *Tea Party* embodies the values that the vast majority of us hold dear, and we are no longer willing to sit idly by, watching those who apparently "know better" (Jon Stewart? Keith Olbermann? *David Letterman? Paris Hilton?*) *tear down our country and our "outmoded" values.* Do *they* represent *your* values? I ask you: *When did freedom go out of style?*

We have just awakened of late to the fact that *the abuses* of those whom we elect (and pay) to represent us, as well as an army of unelected bureaucrats (whom we also pay at a rate including benefits that is twice that which we on average receive: $123K vs. $61K – http://www.investorsinsight.com/blogs/forecasts_trends/archive/2010/08/17/federal-workers-make-twice-that-of-private-sector.aspx), *have all but suffocated us* – as well as our economy. So, in case you are wondering, the *Tea Party* movement *represents the America that most of us grew up in*...and we *aren't* going to let it go!

For those who claim to "love it," but want to "fundamentally transform it," imagine how your spouse would react if you were to say those two things to him or her. *"I 'love you,' Dear, but I feel the need to 'fundamentally transform' you."* Try that when you get home tonight, and let me know how it goes! (My thanks to Glenn Beck for that clear-thinking analogy!) This is a perfect example of an outrageous assertion that *not only went completely unchallenged by the media*, but was likely hailed as "brilliant." The use of that very term was used *ad nauseum* to describe the selection of a General who appeared to be the only possible pick. (*Google* "Obama choice of McCrystal brilliant.")

Yes, there are in this country, as in every country in the world, those living in poverty, but this *was* the one country on earth in which people had the opportunity to work their way out of poverty, as so many of all races and nationalities have done. *That* is the very story of America! If we continue to "level the playing field," however, we will soon be poor across the board, with no opportunity – or incentive – to better our circumstances, along with those of our fellow beings, both here and in much of the rest of the world!

Now, thankfully, we have *numerous* means of "getting the score," and we therefore *know* that we are not alone – *in fact*, we are the majority. Michael Moore (*Capitalism: A Love Story*), Janeane Garafalo (*"This is about hating a black man in the White House. This is racism straight up. That is nothing but a bunch of teabagging rednecks".*), and Katie Couric (*"It might be Islamophobia, Obamaphobia, or both....but we cannot let fear and rage tear down the towers of our core American values."*) dismiss and disdain those of us in the *true mainstream, who do not share their globalist world view.*

The celebs and their media cohorts do not represent the "average" American. *They*, in fact, *are the fringe*, and have always been so...and rather than wonder if *others* believe this, I suggest you ask only if *you* know it to be true. In fact, if you will listen to your own heart – rather than what "others" are saying – you will *know* that you have known this all along. In truth, *most* of the "values" that "society" (the world) has taught you (wealth as the highest priority, "sophistication," overt sexuality, political correctness in general – basically, anything that you were taught was wrong when you were growing up) are not values at all...and *you* know it!

So stop listening to "the world," and *start listening to your own inner voice* – the voice of your Creator. If we as a nation will do this, we will return the country to its previous greatness. However, whether anyone else does, or not, what matters most is that *you and I do it ourselves*. If we do, *we* at least guarantee *our own peace and happiness*. (A good place to start is with Glenn Beck's *Forty-Day Challenge,* at www.glennbeck.com.)

To those who may believe that religion and morality have no bearing on freedom, or that they should be excluded from a discussion of government, I refer them once more to our founders:

"Our Constitution was made only for a moral and religious people. It is wholly inadequate to the government of any other."

John Adams – *to the Officers of the First Brigade of the Third Division of the Militia of Massachusetts* - October 11, 1798

http://www.beliefnet.com/resourcelib/docs/115/Message_from_John_Adams_to_the_Officers_of_the_First_Brigade_1.html

"Only a virtuous people are capable of freedom. As nations become corrupt and vicious, they have more need of masters."

Ben Franklin – *To the Abbés Chalut and Arnoux – April 17, 1787*
http://franklinpapers.org/franklin/framedVolumes.jsp

"We have staked the whole future of American civilization, not upon the power of government, far from it. We've staked the future of all our political institutions upon our capacity...to sustain ourselves according to the Ten Commandments of God."

James Madison – 1778 – *To the General Assembly of the State of Virginia*
http://www.seekfind.net/Feedback__We_have_staked_the_whole_future.html

In every conflict there are those who line up on opposite sides of the struggle. There are, of course, those who try to remain in the middle, but they soon disgrace themselves to both their fellow beings and their posterity. As the English *Jurist*, Sir Edmund Burke, once said, *"All that is necessary for evil to triumph is for good men to do nothing."* Thomas Jefferson added: *"All tyranny needs to gain a foothold is for people of good conscience to remain silent."*

And so I add my voice to the chorus of those who refuse to sit idly by and watch the country and the *Constitution* that we love "fundamentally transformed" before our eyes – while many of our fellow countrymen still slumber, apparently mesmerized by the elite media into thinking that to defend freedom or oppose tyranny is either passé or extreme. Some have even called it "seditious" (Joe Klein, of *Time* magazine, speaking of Sarah Palin and Glenn Beck: http://www.politico.com/news/stories/0410/36020.html).

Indeed, *"If this be [seditious, let us] make the most of it!"*

Patrick Henry (paraphrased)–*Speech to the Virginia Assembly–May 30, 1765*

I am confident that the "average" and "ordinary" (*extra*ordinary, actually) people of this country will rise up and throw off the chains with which we have been steadily bound over the past one-hundred years by both Democrats and Republicans. We will not *"return to the 'pre-stimulus' spending of 2008"!* To do so would be to spray *Bactine* (antiseptic) on a gaping wound, *when only major surgery will save us!*

We must *and we will* return to the limited Constitutional rule which prevented the usurpation of the power of the people to govern and regulate their own lives; and we will create once more real and sustainable wealth for millions of Americans – *not by initiating any new government program*, but by *banishing the government* from the free market, *except where its presence is specifically authorized by our Constitution – and that is a very limited sphere!*

When the Pilgrims arrived on our shores at Plymouth Rock, they had no *safety net!* They had no *health care!* They had no guarantees of worldly success (other than those found in *the Word, so happily referenced recently by our current House Speaker*). They did have three things, however: *freedom* to build their own lives; *determination*, that through effort and hard work they could and would succeed; and *faith* in themselves and their God. And, somehow, without the aid of an "all-caring," and *all-powerful* government, they managed to forge out of the wilderness *the freest and most prosperous nation that has ever existed on planet Earth!*

Somehow we have, since then, become so "advanced" or "sophisticated" as to no longer believe that initiative, hard work, and self-reliance – as well as reliance on our families, our churches, our communities, and our God – are adequate to our survival and/or our success. *We must reject this notion!* Truth is unchanging, and the principles that made this nation great have not, *and will not* change! We simply need to re-enthrone them, and remove the crushing weight of the government (at *every* level) from the backs of those Americans willing to work to realize the dreams of *their own choosing!*

"Those who would give up Essential Liberty to purchase a little Temporary Safety deserve neither Liberty nor Safety."

Ben Franklin – *from a letter written in 1755 from the Assembly to the Governor of Pennsylvania.*

http://en.wikipedia.org/wiki/Those_who_would_give_up_Essential_Liberty

"If a nation values anything more than freedom, it will lose its freedom; and the irony of it is that, if it is comfort or money it values more, it will lose that too."

William Somerset Maugham – in *Strictly Personal*, Chapter 31 (1941)

America is awakening, and for perhaps the first time in a century, we understand that WE, THE PEOPLE, have the power to *restore* – not *"transform"* – our nation's greatness. Together, *"one nation, under God,"* we will make this happen! In the pages that follow I will articulate *one vision* of how this can be done. This is not a course of action for the timid or the weak, however. *Only the brave, who once again wish to be free, need apply!*

"The issue today is the same as it has been throughout all history, whether man shall be allowed to govern himself or be ruled by a small elite."
Thomas Jefferson

"Where the law of the majority ceases to be acknowledged, there government ends, the law of the strongest takes its place, and life and property are his who can take them."

Thomas Jefferson *to Annapolis Citizens, 1809.* ME 16:337

http://etext.virginia.edu/jefferson/quotations/jeff0500.htm

"I know not what course others may take, but as for me, give me liberty or give me death!"

Patrick Henry – *Speech to Virginia Convention* – March 23, 1775

http://www.history.org/almanack/people/bios/biohen.cfm

"And for the support of this Declaration, with a firm reliance on the protection of divine Providence, we mutually pledge to each other our Lives, our Fortunes, and our sacred Honor."

Thomas Jefferson - and Signers of the *Declaration of Independence*

http://www.ushistory.org/declaration/document/

Chapter Six

The Lens of *Truth*

"The world will little note, nor long remember what we say here, but it can never forget what they did here. It is for us the living, rather, to be dedicated here to the unfinished work which they who fought here have thus far so nobly advanced. It is rather for us to be here dedicated to the great task remaining before us -- that from these honored dead we take increased devotion to that cause for which they gave the last full measure of devotion -- that we here highly resolve that these dead shall not have died in vain -- that this nation, under God, shall have a new birth of freedom -- and that government of the people, by the people, for the people, shall not perish from the earth."

Abraham Lincoln – *Gettysburg Address*

"We hold these truths to be self-evident, that all men are created equal, that they are endowed by their Creator with certain unalienable Rights, that among these are Life, Liberty and the pursuit of Happiness. — That to secure these rights, Governments are instituted among Men, deriving their just powers from the consent of the governed...."

Thomas Jefferson – *Declaration of Independence*

"The will of the people is the only legitimate foundation of any government, and to protect its free expression should be our first object."

Thomas Jefferson – *Letter to Benjamin Waring, 1801.* ME 10:236

I begin with these quotes because they articulate the true nature of the struggle in which we are engaged. Simply put, it is the struggle between liberty and oppression, and while the latter is now and has throughout history been disguised and defended as benevolence or compassion, it is by its very nature evil. Thus the struggle is, as it has been from the time of Eden, the struggle between good and evil.

As has been the case for time immemorial, there are a self-selected few who assert that they are better qualified to rule over us than we are to rule ourselves. It is their "responsibility," they say, to provide us with a "safety net" to prevent us not only from *failing*, but also from *suffering – or even struggling*, apparently!

"Good intentions will always be pleaded for every assumption of authority. It is hardly too strong to say that the Constitution was made to guard the people against the dangers of good intentions. There are men in all ages who mean to govern well, but they mean to govern. They promise to be good masters, but they intend to be masters."

Daniel Webster

They speak always of those who *"can't take care of themselves,"* and thus, over the years, they have succeeded in creating a victim class who "know" that in this, *the once-freest nation in all of history*, they could never make it on their own – *primarily because of those who allegedly use and oppress them*. The oppressors are, of course, the "evil rich" – who also *employ them*, and, by so doing, feed both their own families and the families of those whom they employ...as well as *oppress!* Because through greater intellect, talent, or effort *they have achieved more* than others – who are *often* far better off than the average person in much of the rest of the world – *those with less* are taught to envy and even hate them because of their wealth and their success.

Thus many have grown up "understanding" full well that one party is "the party of the rich," while the other is "for the working man or woman," and with this world view they see and interpret every position or proposed piece of legislation as being "for the rich," and "against the poor" – or "the elderly," or...you supply the class. *They can never make it* because of those evil rich *and their party!*

As absurd as this is, once one has accepted these premises as fact – that one party is *'only for the (evil) rich,'* while the other is *'for the poor or working class'* – and has learned to wallow in his or her misery (*which is continuously reported as being caused by the rich*), he cannot possibly draw truthful conclusions! He or she sees *everything* through the lens of oppression and class warfare.

The same is true of the "victims" of race. All is seen – and subsequently *experienced* – through the lens of race and racism; and like most everything else in life, this becomes a self-fulfilling prophecy. (See my previous book, *The Secret of Life*, Millennium Publishing, 2009.)

Those looking for racism, or inequality – *or unfairness of any kind* – will surely find it. One need only look to the recent example of the "cracker hater," King Samir Shabazz, one of the *New Black Panthers* (pardoned by the "Justice" Department after threatening voters at a Chicago polling place during the last presidential election), seen spewing his own racist hatred at those who have *"caused him"* to live in a (self-made) prison of powerlessness and poverty. He even openly advocates "killing some cracker babies!"
(http://www.youtube.com/watch?v=lDsTvKvV_hg).

We can only pray for those who see (and subsequently *experience*) only hatred and bigotry, *but not the opportunity, and the need, to rise above it* – if only for one's self, if for no one else!

In all of life there is a choice, to wallow in misery, or to seek to break free of it. What would have become of the homeless father, Chris Gardener, living on the streets of San Francisco (*The Pursuit of Happyness*), and countless others who started with nothing, *if he and they had chosen to focus on all that was wrong with, and all that was unfair about their lives and their country?* How many people has Michael Moore inspired to rise above their circumstances and find true happiness? *Is there any doubt in your mind as to the answer?*

The scripture says that "The light of the body is the eye: if therefore thine eye be single [not duplicitous], thy whole body shall be full of light. But if thine eye be evil [or untruthful], thy whole body shall be full of darkness! If therefore the light that is in thee be darkness, how great is that darkness!" (Matthew 6: 22-23).

This is simply another way of saying that *if your perspective or point of view* – your "eye," or the way you see things – *is evil*, or you are seeing things through an untruthful or dishonest (or even just mistaken) lens, then everything you "see" will be darkness – "and how great is that darkness!"

Everything that you see through the lens of deceit will be darkness; and you will be unable to judge anything with exactitude, but will see and judge everything incorrectly. Your conclusions will be "logical," *but false in every instance,* because the *premises* upon which you are basing them are false. We must see through the lens of truth!

The one party is *not* 'for the poor,' and the other is not *only* 'for the rich.' One is for big government *and extensive control and regulation* – and the oppressive taxation that they necessitate – and the other is at least *supposed to be* for maximum freedom and the prosperity that results therefrom...*not for the rich*, but *for everyone*; so that all can be rich if they so choose and *have the God-given ability to achieve it*; but no one is preventing them by *their own* success. *Everyone's honest success is to everyone else's benefit.*

I say "supposed to be" in referring to the Republicans, because many of them clearly are not. True conservatives, however, are *absolutely for maximum freedom for the individual*, and therefore, for small government.

Ironically, while most of those in the "working class" (*as if in order to be successful or wealthy one didn't have to work or put forth any effort*), who see everything through the 'dark glass' of party, *were* at one time (if not *still*) brought up in the church, they seem to have forgotten the divine directive to "not covet" one's neighbor's property or possessions. They, as well as those on the "other side" who only see things from the perspective of party, seem also to look the other way when those who pretend to represent them "misrepresent" the facts in an effort to justify their positions.

Witness the current incessant mantra that the woeful state of the economy is the fault of the previous Administration. Any honest observer must decry the excessive spending of both the former White House and the Congress – which was under the same leadership during the last two years of the previous Administration as it is now. The deficit in 2008, the last year of the former Administration (and second year for the Democratically-lead Congress) was a record $457 Billion – and that is with *Enron*-like accounting! (See: http://www.heritage.org/research/reports/2006/06/federal-budget-should-include-long-term-obligations-from-entitlement-programs).

The *reported* federal deficit during 2009, the first year of the current Administration, and third year for the Democratically-lead Congress, was $1.41 Trillion – triple that of the previous administration's record-breaking deficit. The CBO, however, had estimated that the deficit for that year would be $1.2 Trillion even before the current president took office. (I'm sure the current White House had *nothing* to do with that!)

The deficit for the current year (which just expired) was projected to reach $1.47 Trillion, higher still, and $1.42 Trillion in 2011. *Obviously, each of these deficits represents a dramatic increase in spending*, so to blame our current economic woes on the spending and policies of the previous Administration is a stretch at best, and blatantly dishonest at worst.

While those on the Left blame the tax cuts of the former President and Congress for the current "recession," as is usually the case, the real culprit was – and *is* - spending. The tax revenues since the tax cuts were implemented have actually exceeded the 20, 40, and 60 year historical averages, and "The inflation-adjusted 20 percent tax revenue increase between 2004 and 2006 represents the largest two-year revenue surge since 1965-1967." (*Heritage Foundation – "Ten Myths about the Bush Tax Cuts,"* January 29, 2007, by Brian Riedl – [2] Office of Management and Budget, *Historical Tables, Budget of the United States Government, Fiscal Year 2007* (Washington, D.C.: U.S. Government Printing Office, 2006), pp. 25–26, Table 1.3, at
www.whitehouse.gov/omb/budget/fy2007/pdf/hist.pdf (January 16, 2007)).

Not unsurprisingly, this type of rhetoric was also forbidden in the *Decalogue,* or *Ten Commandments*, and has even been referenced recently by the current occupant of the White House while chastising those who were seeking to block yet another in a long list of his abuses of power. In a classic example of projecting one's own *modus operandi* on others, he admonished: "*Thou shalt not bear false witness!*"

Thus, for example, when for solely political gain, the President, or his party, label those who oppose illegal immigration as "anti-immigrant," they are not simply being "disingenuous" (a term the media conjured up in the not too distant past in order to provide cover for one of their own), they are prevaricating – or, in a word, *lying*.

Sadly, it is completely lost on those who unquestioningly buy the lies and rhetoric of the "benevolent benefactors of the oppressed," *who somehow grow exceedingly wealthy themselves, while "serving" their "poor" constituents*, that there are ever growing numbers of both the poor and the oppressed – *in spite of extensive taxation and regulation*. In other words, all of the taxing, spending, regulating, and litigating, have had no beneficial effect on poverty other than lowering the standard of living for all (and creating a welfare and entitlement state for millions who "can't afford" to work!). From the world view of the caretakers of the poor and oppressed, however, bringing down the rich – as well as the middle class – *is, at the very least, fair!*

So I ask you: Do such attitudes represent your values? Is this the kind of country in which you wish (*choose*) to live? This is all, of course, conveniently blamed on "the rich" or "the party of the rich," and the obvious solution, they say, is more legislation, more regulation, and, of necessity, more taxation. All of which further weakens the economy and the business climate in which we all work and live – *"rich" and "poor" alike.* The economy is the ocean upon which all ships either rise or fall. It cannot be otherwise. Some ships may be suited to travel farther or faster, but *all* rise or fall with the tide!

Isn't it time that we forget about *parties,* and 'winning at all costs,' and simply start doing *what is right for America and its people?* I saw a rather nice ad on TV earlier today, but I take exception with two things that it said. It called for a *"more caring government,"* and one that *"remembers us."*

It is not the role of government to "be caring" or to "care *for*" any of us – *as you will soon see!*

I do not want a government that *"remembers"* me. I want a government that understands perfectly well that it *belongs* to me – *and to all of us!*

Chapter Seven

The Legal Limits of *Government!*

Perhaps the most insidious and deceitful thing that our elected "representatives" do to us is to hide the truth – in other words, *lie to us!* It is as if we are children, who cannot "handle" the truth. Once again, it is amazing how just the simple directives that thundered down from *Mt. Sinai* have such a profound effect on each of us, and on our society as a whole – *especially when we do not follow them!*

The "conventional wisdom" is that "the public" "can't take" this or that. So, the "advisors" to the presidents tell them to say such and such – *but not the truth*. Once one begins to go down this path – and it is one that we as a country have been on for as long as any of us can remember, and no doubt longer still – then the entire one-way "dialogue" is only an endless string of platitudes that our "leaders" think we want or need to hear. *Anything but the truth!*

This can only have one result, and that is that we have no idea – and *no way of knowing for sure* in most cases – whether or not what we are being told is true...*but we're fairly certain, most of the time, that it's not!* And that is precisely the state in which we currently find ourselves; but as I have said, *this has been the practice of politicians* – they can't possibly be called *leaders* while continually under the "necessity" of *mis*-leading those they allegedly "serve" – as I was saying, this has been the practice of politicians *"forever"* (in the vernacular).

So, we have been told for some time that it is the role of government to "take care of us!" (I was in a meeting some years ago in which the speaker, a council woman, started out by saying: *"As you know, it's our job to take care of our constituents."* I immediately "begged to differ!") It sounded wonderful, of course, but who did she think she was? Did we, as adults, *want* or *need* her to "take care of" us? Of course not!

It is not the job of government to be *"more caring!"* It is not the place of the government – *nor does it have the authority* – to care for any among us. That is our job, and the job of our families, churches, and private charities – especially those based in our local communities. It is *not* the role of government!

I often hear even the most ardent "conservative" (even *Libertarian*) pundits say things like, *"Of course, we have to take care of those who can't take care of themselves."* It sounds good, and may make them look kind and charitable, but it is patently false, and *completely counter to the rule of law!* You heard me right. (*Keep reading!*)

Should we be charitable? Absolutely! Should we be forced to be? Absolutely *not!* We have been duped into thinking that this is the proper role of government. It is not – even though every "news" commentator, "celebrity," and college professor to whom you have ever listened has told you that it is! In a word, they were *wrong!*

By way of reminder, I will ask you once again to not "wonder," or *care,* what others might think of this. Just read on, and listen to the words of several of our founders and past presidents regarding the role of the government in matters of charity. Keep in mind that the *inspired* wisdom of our founders was such that they were able to establish a system of government that resulted in the most prosperity and freedom, for the greatest number of people, of any system ever devised. The systems now trumpeted by the "other side" can claim no such success – *anywhere in history (past or present)!*

I say "trumpeted," but obfuscation (obscuring one's true intentions) is almost always the *M.O. YouTube* and the *Internet* have made it a bit difficult for them to hide the entire record, but the elitist media does a yeoman's job of suppressing any *faux pas.* Unfortunately for them, however, but fortunately for us, the majority now get their "news" elsewhere!

First, from the *"Father"* of the *Declaration –*

"The moment the idea is admitted into society that property is not as sacred as the laws of God, and that there is not a force of law and public justice to protect it, anarchy and tyranny commence. If 'Thou shalt not covet' and 'Thou shalt not steal' were not commandments of Heaven, they must be made inviolable precepts in every society before it can be civilized or made free."

John Adams – *A Defense of the* Constitutions *of Government of the United States of America, 1787*

Next, from the *author* of the *Declaration* -

"When all government, domestic and foreign, in little as in great things, shall be drawn to Washington as the center of all power, it will render powerless the checks provided of one government on another and will become as venal and oppressive as the government from which we separated."

Thomas Jefferson – to Charles Hammond, 1821. *The Writings of Thomas Jefferson*, (Memorial Edition) Lipscomb and Bergh, editors, ME 15:332

And finally (from the *Founders*), the *"Father"* of the Constitution –

In 1794, when Congress appropriated $15,000 for relief of French refugees who fled from insurrection in San Domingo to Baltimore and Philadelphia, James Madison stood on the floor of the House to object saying, *"I cannot undertake to lay my finger on that article of the Constitution which granted a right to Congress of expending, on objects of benevolence, the money of their constituents."*

James Madison – 4 Annals of congress 179 (1794)

http://conservativecolloquium.wordpress.com/2007/11/24/founding-fathers-on-charity-wealth-redistribution-and-federal-govt/

"[T]he government of the United States is a definite government, confined to specified objects. It is not like the state governments, whose powers are more general. Charity is no part of the legislative duty of the government."

James Madison – *Annals of Congress, House of Representatives, 3rd Congress, 1st Session, page 170*

It will be noted that these are not simply *signers* of the *Declaration*, or of the Constitution, *but, rather, three of the four pre-eminent figures in the creation of these, the two key documents upon which our entire system of government is founded* – Franklin being the fourth.

As promised, here are several other quotes from some of our past presidents:

"I can find no warrant for such an appropriation in the Constitution, and I do not believe that the power and duty of the General Government ought to be extended to the relief of individual suffering which is in no manner properly related to the public service or benefit."

President Grover Cleveland vetoing a bill for charity relief (18 Congressional Record 1875 [1877])

"I cannot find any authority in the Constitution for public charity. [To approve the measure] would be contrary to the letter and spirit of the Constitution and subversive to the whole theory upon which the Union of these States is founded."

President Franklin Pierce's 1854 veto of a measure to help the mentally ill

"The friendliness and charity of our countrymen can always be relied upon to relieve their fellow citizens in misfortune. This has been repeatedly and quite lately demonstrated. Federal aid in such cases encourages the expectation of paternal care on the part of the Government and weakens the sturdiness of our national character, while it prevents the indulgence among our people of that kindly sentiment and conduct which strengthens the bonds of a common brotherhood."

President Herbert Hoover – The President's News Conference, February 3, 1931

http://www.presidency.ucsb.edu/ws/index.php?pid=22932

President Grover Cleveland, in 1887, confronted with a similar issue stated in part:

"A prevalent tendency to disregard the limited mission of this power and duty should, I think, be steadfastly resisted, to the end that the lesson should be constantly enforced that though the people support the Government, the Government should not support the people."

http://www.mackinac.org/7440

While I do not wish to belabor this point, it is pivotal to the entire question of whether we will maintain an adherence to the *Constitution* and the Rule of Law, or will allow ourselves as a nation to be severed from our legal foundation, *and become a nation of men, and not of laws* – in direct opposition to the timeless principles upon which our country was founded. This is not *an* issue. It is *the* issue, *and has been throughout the ages!*

In 1787, in the *"miracle at Philadelphia,"* our Founders set up the greatest and most successful experiment in self-government to ever be conducted. Because it could not guarantee an identical outcome to every member of society, some choose to focus only on the inequities and failings of our system, rather than on its unprecedented success. They claim to "love" America, but what does that mean?

Michael Moore, an ardent spokesman of the Left, has recently produced a movie called *Capitalism: A Love Affair.* While I have no plans to contribute to his hypocritical accrual of wealth in this "evil" capitalist system which has enabled him to "earn" millions by attacking its "inherent unfairness," it is clearly an attempt to mock those of us enamored with the idea of bettering ourselves and our circumstances through the freedom to choose and pursue our own path – no doubt the very things which he has done. So what exactly is it that he loves – the geography? Certainly it can't be any of the evil "things" – cars, clothes, technology, etc. – that *capitalism* has produced! (In a "word," this is textbook liberal hypocrisy!)

Fortunately for both Michael Moore and the country as a whole, the vast majority of Americans, who really do love their country, completely reject his world view, and recognize the overt hypocrisy and intellectual dishonesty of his philosophy and "love of country."

I will now conclude with one last statement regarding the government's "role" in alleviating the sufferings of its citizens. As I write this I am reminded – and wish to remind you – that *government* has no money. Any money that it presumes to have and "give" to others is only money that it *takes* from us. Since it has only limited authority to do a few specified ("enumerated") things, and has no legal authority to do anything not so specified, then when it presumes to tax its citizens to do more than *they* have granted it permission to do, *it violates the fundamental/highest law of the land!*

By way of explanation – and *recommendation* – I urge any honest seeker of truth regarding the role of the government in dispensing aid to those in need, to read the story that surrounded the issuance of the statement made below. It is one of the most inspiring stories you will ever read about an individual citizen and his influence on both the legendary Congressman who made the statement, and on the many who knew this highly-principled and highly-informed man. The full account can be read at: http://www.lewrockwell.com/orig4/ellis1.html.

"Mr. Speaker--I have as much respect for the memory of the deceased, and as much sympathy for the sufferings of the living, if suffering there be, as any man in this House, but we must not permit our respect for the dead or our sympathy for a part of the living to lead us into an act of injustice to the balance of the living. I will not go into an argument to prove that Congress has not the power to appropriate this money as an act of charity. Every member upon this floor knows it. We have the right, as individuals, to give away as much of our own money as we please in charity; but as members of Congress we have no right so to appropriate a dollar of the public money."
Congressman Davy Crockett, of Tennessee - *Originally published in "The Life of Colonel David Crockett," by Edward Sylvester Ellis, 1861.*
(Please read the full account at: http://www.lewrockwell.com/orig4/ellis1.html.)

With apologies, I must add one more, this one from perhaps the wisest citizen in our nation's history:
"I am for doing good to the poor, but I differ in opinion of the means. I think the best way of doing good to the poor, is not making them easy in poverty, but leading or driving them out of it. In my youth I travelled much, and I observed in different countries, that the more public provisions were made for the poor, the less they provided for themselves, and of course became poorer. And, on the contrary, the less was done for them, the more they did for themselves, and became richer."

Benjamin Franklin - *On the Price of Corn and Management of the Poor, November 1766*

A less wise person could (and will, no doubt) simply respond by saying that this is a calloused and insensitive remark – without *getting* (or admitting to) the bottom line – that being that *the beneficiaries of this approach were the poor themselves!* Thus, a truly *compassionate* person *would* insist on it! Results *should* matter!

Chapter Eight

The Classless Instigators of Class Warfare

Another "dirty little secret" is that *there is no such thing as a corporate tax*. Whatever taxes a corporation must pay, must, in the end, be paid by those who purchase their products – and those who can least afford the higher prices that are the result of taxing the "evil corporations" are the very "poor" whom the repressive legislation and its benighted sponsors pretend to "serve."

And they either know this, or, because their eye is duplicitous, or not "single" (*being blinded by ambition, or allegiance to party*), they are *incapable* of seeing what is plain to all who have chosen not to 'walk in darkness at noonday' – that is to say, *to live* in the (once) freest and, *not coincidentally*, most prosperous nation on earth, while seeing only its failures, and, while being wildly wealthy themselves (whilst working in this same "oppressive" system), seek only to ridicule and tear it down.

Meanwhile, in an economy decimated by government interference in a free market system that has clearly made us the envy of the world (most of which is *not free* to achieve such wealth), our politicians, normally enamored with regulation and taxation, instinctively know that for *themselves* and the economy to survive, *they must reduce taxes* – or, at least, *not raise them*; this after years (including the present one) of denouncing these same lower tax rates as "crippling" the economy. When their careers are at stake, however, *they suddenly "get religion,"* and do what they inwardly (at the very least) knew was best for the country all along.

While this may be the height of hypocrisy, it is "business as usual" for those who traffic in *blaming the rich for all that ails us*. It is the same "class warfare" that has been employed by tyrants throughout the ages, pitting one group against another for the purpose of solidifying their power base. This has little to do with "the poor," but *everything* to do with their self-appointed caretakers!

In spite of this obvious fact, these same politicians – and, make no mistake, *that is all that they are* – these same politicians *steadfastly refuse to lower taxes on "the rich,"* even though doing so would clearly benefit the economy as a whole, *to the benefit of everyone in society*, including the poor whom they purport to represent – *because doing so would violate their circus act of class warfare*...blaming the rich for all that is wrong with society.

Nothing, of course, could be further from the truth. Once again, in order to extend or maintain their own wealth and power, they seek to destroy the very ones upon whom the wealth of the nation most depends. Everyone who works contributes, but *without the capital of those who have succeeded and saved, businesses and industries* – and the resulting wealth and employment they engender – *cannot be created*.

While this author thinks it despicable that certain *corporate CEO's* and *corporate executives* earn tens and sometimes *hundreds* of millions of dollars in salaries, perks, and "bonuses," even as their companies falter, it is the "evil" *business owners* of this country – small and large – that provide the jobs and means of support for virtually everyone else in the country.

Since these CEO's may not have risked all to start their companies – as is often the case with business owners (large and small) – their compensation does appear to be excessive. This is the result of a misguided greed that is counter to the virtue and morals that our Founders insisted were necessary to the perpetuation and ultimate survival of our system of political and economic freedom.

"Bad men cannot make good citizens. A vitiated state of morals, a corrupted public conscience are incompatible with freedom."

Patrick Henry
http://www.cancertutor.com/Quotes/Quotes_Presidents.html

"That no free government, or the blessing of liberty, can be preserved to any people but by a firm adherence to justice, moderation, temperance, frugality, and virtue, and by frequent recurrence to fundamental principles."

George Mason, the *Virginia Declaration of Rights*, 1776

"Without morals a republic cannot subsist any length of time; they therefore who are decrying the Christian religion, whose morality is so sublime and pure (and) which insures to the good eternal happiness, are undermining the solid foundation of morals, the best security for the duration of free governments."

Charles Carroll, signer of the *Declaration of Independence The Life and Correspondence of James McHenry* by Bernard C. Steiner 1907, from a letter from Charles Carroll, Nov. 4, 1800

http://www.straight-talk.net/socas/s-views.shtml

I hasten to add, however, that government has *no right* to interfere in proscribing compensation in the marketplace – for either *minimum* wages or maximum salaries as our current Chief Executive has so flagrantly done either this year or last. (For the government to *own*, in full or in part, *any* business is also, of course, *a clear and blatant violation of the limited powers enumerated in the Constitution!*)

"We have no government armed with power capable of contending with human passions unbridled by morality and religion. Avarice, ambition, revenge, or gallantry, would break the strongest cords of our Constitution as a whale goes through a net. Our Constitution was made only for a moral and religious people. It is wholly inadequate to the government of any other."

John Adams (*The Works of John Adams*, ed. C. F. Adams, Boston: Little, Brown Co., 1851, 4:31)
http://cancertutor.com/Quotes/Quotes_Presidents.html

I witnessed just today on television one of the *ruling class* pointing out the *inequities* of our system – thus championing *"redistribution."*

"Now in the last seven years we have had the highest corporate profit ever in American history. Highest corporate profit! We've had the highest productivity! The American worker has produced more per person at any time, but it hasn't been shared, and that's the problem because we have been guided by a republican administration who believes in this simplistic notion that people who have wealth are entitled to keep it and they have an antipathy towards the means of redistributing wealth."

http://virginiavirtucon.wordpress.com/2008/11/04/jim-moran-this-simplistic-notion-that-people-who-have-wealth-are-entitled-to-keep-it/

As I have just pointed out, *I agree* that corporate boards and their CEO's should be guided by virtue and morality in every aspect of their lives – and that includes what is fair in the workplace. However, in making such a statement (on November 4, 2008), Democratic Senator Jim Moran, of Virginia, is clearly articulating that it is the government's place to "solve" the matter by "redistributing wealth." That, of course, is precisely the solution that Karl Marx would have offered in this case.

The writer of the *Declaration* had another take on the matter....

"To take from one, because it is thought his own industry and that of his father's has acquired too much, in order to spare to others, who, or whose fathers, have not exercised equal industry and skill, is to violate arbitrarily the first principle of association, the guarantee to everyone the free exercise of his industry and the fruits acquired by it."

Thomas Jefferson, letter to Joseph Milligan, April 6, 1816

http://conservativecolloquium.wordpress.com/2007/11/24/founding-fathers-on-charity-wealth-redistribution-and-federal-govt/

Poor Richard foresaw another pitfall with this government "solution"–

"When the people find they can vote themselves money, that will herald the end of the republic."

Benjamin Franklin

http://econfaculty.gmu.edu/wew/quotes/govt.html

The *"mainstream"* cheerleaders, all the while masquerading as "reporters," feign disbelief over the label "socialist." As pointed out, however, this career politician, in office since 1991, is echoing the very language of *Das Kapital*. I am not suggesting that he has even read it, but the philosophy is the same – and so would be the result if not checked. The irony here is that while Jim Moran may have no conscious sympathies for Marx and Engels, the current Administration is brim with those who openly proclaim allegiance thereto – even though when questioned they hedge. (See http://www.cnsnews.com/news/article/55665.)

While I have little doubt that Mr. Moran would claim – for his party, at least – credit for the passage of the *Thirteenth Amendment*, and the subsequent *Civil Rights Act* (neither of which would be true), he obviously draws no parallel between the forced confiscation of property, which he so piously demands, and involuntary servitude – which is expressly prohibited by the *Thirteenth Amendment*.

How is this any different from slavery, wherein one group with the power of numbers (as opposed to that of wealth, and the guns *it* will buy) forces another, less powerful group (regardless of their presumed holdings or social status), to do its bidding. *It is not!*

"The majority, oppressing an individual ([or group of individuals)], is guilty of a crime, abuses its strength, and by acting on the law of the strongest breaks up the foundations of society."

Thomas Jefferson

"The sole end for which mankind are warranted, individually or collectively, in interfering with the liberty of action of any of their number, is self-protection."

John Stuart Mill – from essay *On Liberty* (1859)

"The legitimate powers of government extend to [preventing] such acts only as are injurious to others."

Thomas Jefferson, *Notes on Virginia, 1782. The Writings of Thomas Jefferson,* (Memorial Edition) Lipscomb and Bergh, editors, ME 2:221

Chapter Nine

Standing for Truth – *Ignoring* Obfuscation

If one doubts that this is evil, he need only ask any of the enlightened few, who assign to themselves the superior intellect needed to guide – or, let us be clear, *rule* – the masses, how he or she would feel if the tables were turned. Of course the self-selected "guardians" of the people instinctively scoff at the notion that the masses could take care of themselves. *Would they, however, suggest that they are also incapable of casting an informed vote?*

We have been so indoctrinated over the past fifty years by the (wealthy, interestingly) media elites and politicians, on *the evils of profit and wealth* (and free enterprise in general) – as well as the despised corporations (that supply virtually everything we need to sustain our lives and lifestyles) – that most would not dare counter the charges by suggesting that we have the inalienable right to "life, liberty, and the pursuit of happiness," and that it is not the place of those government officials whom we hire (and whose salaries we pay – elected and otherwise), to tell us how we should be spending our time or our money.

"It is the highest impertinence and presumption, therefore, in kings and ministers to pretend to watch over the economy of private people, and to restrain their expense.... They are themselves always, and without any exception, the greatest spendthrifts in society. Let them look well after their own expense, and they may safely trust private people with theirs."

Adam Smith, *An Inquiry into the Nature and Causes of the Wealth of Nations* [1776]

http://econfaculty.gmu.edu/wew/quotes/govt.html

It is my intention here to dismiss such absurd propositions with simple logic and obvious truth. I refuse to check my apparently *un*common sense at the door, in order to appear or "sound like" I am as caring and compassionate as those who presume to lecture "ordinary" people on their own redefined versions of morality.

It may not have escaped your notice that those who stridently condemn any who dare to question the actual morality of certain behaviors or lifestyles (defined as immoral by both men and God for millennia), have, not surprisingly, felt it necessary to create or invent a new "morality" in which tolerance trumps decency, and respect for "diversity" is reserved only to those engaged in aberrant behaviors still offensive to the majority. Thus true *diversity of thought* is taboo!

To be more succinct, I will not pretend to engage in an "honest" debate which is based in obviously flawed and "disingenuous" premises – from which no correct conclusion can ever be drawn. While I am clearly passionate about the principles I am positing herein, I refuse to have a discussion based solely on emotion, with no basis in fact or reason. To do so would be the epitome of intellectual dishonesty. Simple logic demands that premises be facts – not spin, *no matter for how long or how broadly they may have been accepted!*

I also refuse – as should we all – to engage in debate with those who knowingly misrepresent the facts. The most egregious example of this is the current misuse (abuse, actually) of the race card. How is it that opposing a president who is partially of another race, is considered "racist," but voting (90-95%) for a president because he is partially, at least, of one's own race is not?

I saw in a poll just last night that some 91% of those who share half of our President's race "approve" of the job he is doing, while only 35% of those who share the other half do not. "Half" of this poll (the "half" in which roughly a third "disapprove" of him) will be considered as evidence of prejudice, or even racism, while it will never occur to those who draw this conclusion that the "half" voting 9 to 1 "for" is not!

It is abundantly clear that those who oppose this same President are equally passionate in their opposition to the House Speaker and Senate Majority Leader, both of whom are at least partially of a different race from the president. In the case of the Speaker, one must assume that it is simple gender discrimination. Meanwhile, these same "extremist haters" may soon elect the first female president in our nation's history. *This same group has already successfully fielded a higher percentage of female candidates than we have ever before seen in a national election!*

The whole matter is designed to distract us from what should be the substance of the debate! When the same people were wildly opposed to Bill Clinton when he occupied the oval office, was that racism? And what of those who called the previous occupant of the White House "Hitler," were they racist? *Of course not, and neither is the current opposition for the vast majority.* The majority of the country did not let race stop them from voting for the man. "It's the economy, stupid!" Actually, it's much more than that, but you get the idea!

"Patriotism means to stand by the country. It does NOT mean to stand by the President or any other public official save exactly to the degree in which he himself stands by the country. It is patriotic to support him insofar as he efficiently serves the country. It is unpatriotic not to oppose him to the exact extent that by inefficiency or otherwise he fails in his duty to stand by the country."

Theodore Roosevelt

http://cancertutor.com/Quotes/Quotes_Presidents.html

"Celebrities" and media elites have been allowed to define, or *re*define, the language of our culture, and to *re*frame the arguments of our day, even though the once-silent majority continue to hold traditional American values, which diverge sharply from the new lexicon of acceptable terms and behaviors. They have even carried this to the *ultimum absurdum* of presuming to dictate how those of us not so "blessed" with compassion and intellect *should think and even feel!*

We now have – at both public and private institutions – mandatory "sensitivity training," not unlike the forced indoctrination employed by totalitarian dictators. This misguided attempt to police our thoughts finds its ultimate expression in the "legal" construct known as "hate-crime legislation" – which makes crimes against favored classes more egregious than those committed against what can only be assumed to be "normal" people, or at least those not "favored."

This compassionate legislation is proffered as a "protection" of the oppressed, but in reality it only serves as a tool to oppress the alleged "oppressors." What was it that that outmoded document (the *Constitution*) had to say about "equal protection" under the law?

Thus if a white were to murder a black (or other "minority" – women, who make up 50+% of the population are universally considered a "minority" by those who traffic in this sort of *doublespeak*), and it were "proven" to be "race-based," or "racially-motivated," he or she would be punished more severely than if a black murdered a black – *even though black-on-black crime is a far greater issue than white-on-black crime. Nonetheless, this new ideology is considered by its proponents – or non-thinking party devotees – as so morally superior that it even trumps the apparently outmoded concepts embodied in the First Amendment!*

If, by chance, you were unaware of the fact, courts in Sweden and elsewhere have already handed down sentences against ministers for engaging in *"hate speech,"* when they have spoken out against homosexuality on Biblical and moral grounds...but certainly that could never happen here! *Right!* (See: http://www.truthtellers.org/hate%20crimes/hatecrimesarticle.html.)

"The jaws of power are always open to devour, and her arm is always stretched out, if possible, to destroy the freedom of thinking, speaking, and writing."

John Adams

http://cancertutor.com/Quotes/Quotes_Presidents.html

Chapter Ten

The Origin of Our Rights...*and the solution to our problems!*

In our day, I often hear "spokesmen" of the people express their "*frustration*" over the state of our nation. *I reject that sentiment!* To accept it would be to imply that we either don't know what the problem is, or that we don't know how to solve it...or, that we are powerless to affect - or *effect* - the desired outcome. *None of this is true!*

We know what the problem is, and we know how to solve it. While it is true that there are several problems, it is readily apparent that each of these stems from the same root cause; and that cause is government itself – not the *limited* government envisioned by our founders, and specifically delineated and authorized by the *Constitution* which they penned, but the bloated, *illegal* bureaucracy that has been allowed to grow unchecked, like a cancer; which – if not eradicated – will ultimately destroy our republic...as it is at this moment threatening to do. *We must act now!*

I do not use the term *"illegal"* unadvisedly, as our founders *emphatically* intended - and *established* - a *limited* government with enumerated [specifically identified] powers, and made it absolutely clear that "The powers not delegated to the United States by the *Constitution*, nor prohibited by it to the States, are reserved to the States respectively, or [in other words] to the people (*Amendment X*)."

"I consider the foundation of the [Federal] Constitution as laid on this ground: That "all powers not delegated to the United States, by the Constitution, nor prohibited by it to the States, are reserved to the States or to the people." [10th Amendment] To take a single step beyond the boundaries thus specifically drawn around the powers of Congress is to take possession of a boundless field of power, no longer susceptible of any definition."

Thomas Jefferson, *"Opinion on the Constitutionality of a National Bank"* February 15, 1791

"We must confine ourselves to the powers described in the Constitution, and the moment we pass it, we take an arbitrary stride towards a despotic Government."

James Jackson, First Congress, *1st Annals of Congress, 489*

"Congress has not unlimited powers to provide for the general welfare, but only those specifically enumerated."

Thomas Jefferson, *Letter to Albert Gallatin, 1817*

http://econfaculty.gmu.edu/wew/quotes/govt.html

Amendment IX underscores the intent of the *Constitution* to *protect our* God-given rights, while clearly proscribing or *limiting* the authority and reach – as well as *purview* – of the government: "The enumeration in the *Constitution*, of certain rights, shall not be construed [or *mis*construed] to deny or disparage other [rights] retained by the people."

Let it here be noted that under the *Constitution, government has no rights!* Government only exists as an extension of the will – and delegated authority - of the people, in order to provide, under their authority, certain limited protections or safeguards to their individual liberties. Our "inalienable rights" do not come from men or from governments as some have recently – and publicly – presumed...and misguidedly proclaimed!

Reference Senator Tom Harkin of Iowa, gleefully proclaiming in perhaps the first truly public discussion (announcement, actually) of the matter in weeks – as it was being concocted behind closed doors – how Congress had *"created a new 'right' for the people,"* after a *hostile take-over* of our nation's healthcare system, against the clearly expressed will of the majority of the American people!

All legitimate rights are natural rights, and they come from our Creator. (While our form of government is unique among men, our rights and freedoms were not "made in America" – although they may have first been seen in 'full bloom' here. They were "made," or originated, before the world was created.)

> "You have rights antecedent to all earthly governments; rights that cannot be repealed or restrained by human laws; right derived from the Great Legislator of the Universe."
>
> John Adams

Let it also be here said that because our inalienable rights accrue from God, *they cannot be taken away by man through any process "legal" or otherwise;* nor can the majority take away the inalienable rights of any citizen or group of citizens.

> "The whole of the Bill (of Rights) is a declaration of the right of the people at large or considered as individuals .... It establishes [(declares)] some rights of the individual as unalienable and which consequently, no majority has a right to deprive them of."
>
> Albert Gallatin, *New York Historical Society*, October 7, 1789

Let me also here remind the *many* who have forgotten – whether by lapse of memory or by a cavalier disregard for the rule of law, as in the case of the ruling class – that the *Constitution* is, *in the most binding legal sense, the Supreme Law of the Land*. While it should go without saying – but *sadly* does not – this unequivocally means that there is *no higher law or authority*; and if any elected (or appointed) "representative" of the people acts contrary to this supreme law, he (or she) violates his (or her) oath of office (to uphold the *Constitution*).

I must also note that it appears obvious that the majority of public officials, including those at the highest levels of government, *all of whom* have sworn to uphold the *Constitution*, have either not read the abundant writings produced by those who created it (which define and explain their true intent in the most pristine terms possible), or they simply have no intention of keeping their oath!

Let me now state clearly that the root cause of every problem we face as a nation is the abandonment of both the *letter* and the *spirit* of the *Constitution* and the *Declaration* (as well as the *Ten Commandments*). Make no mistake, governmentally, at least, the solutions will *all* be found in the *Constitution* and the *Declaration!*

Let me repeat that:

The root cause of every problem we face as a nation [as relates to government] is the abandonment of both the letter and the spirit of the Constitution and the Declaration.

It would seem that this was not an accident on the part of those who have openly challenged the spirit and the intent of the *Constitution* and its authors. Surely it was no accident that so many prominent law schools over the past one hundred years, have not taught the *Constitution* as the legal foundation for all of our laws.

Rather, they have taught *case law*. By taking this approach, they have been able to turn certain safeguards – notably among which is the concept of "freedom of religion," guaranteed by the First Amendment – on their heads. In the case in point, *God* has been virtually *banned* from government, schools, and the public square – by citing the very provision that was unarguably put in place to prevent the infringement of the right of free religious expression.

While it may no longer be played in this day of cell phones and *IM* (Instant Messaging), there was once a popular game, which many will recall, wherein those participating would sit in a circle, and the leader would start by whispering a story to his neighbor; whereupon he would pass it along to *his* neighbor, and so forth, until it had gone full circle. Typically, this resulted in the original message and many of its details being altered – often almost beyond recognition.

It is because of this very likelihood that we should always – in studying the law (as well as history) – return to original sources. When we do not, the results are predictable...and that is precisely where we find ourselves today. Whether this was accidental or intentional – as I have alleged – may matter little in the end, as the result is the same. Our government and its enormous reach today would be entirely unrecognizable to the authors of the *Declaration* and the *Constitution!*

A current "representative of the people" – a *politician*, frankly – openly stated recently (in a live TV interview) that *"There's nothing in the Constitution that says that the federal government has anything to do with most of the stuff we do."* Don't be alarmed, however, Representative James Clyburn is only the third ranking Democrat in the *U.S. House of Representatives*....

He wasn't about to be bested, though, and retorted swiftly: *"How about [you] show me where in the Constitution it prohibits the federal government from doing this?"* [We could start with the 10th Amendment!]

http://www.theamericanview.com/index.php?id=1465

While it was a stunning admission (and frankly pathetic defense), what was most disturbing was that this "representative" saw no inconsistency with the reality he was acknowledging – that *our nations "lawmakers" have little, if any, regard for the law itself*...or, at least, *the law upon which all others are to be legally based!*

Beyond the disregard, however, the thing that was *truly most disturbing* was that he (and, one assumes, his cohorts) could occupy such positions of influence, and not have even the remotest understanding of the *Constitution*, or the foundational principles upon which the entire structure of our government is built!

As for knowing what to do about our current circumstance, I proffer that in clearly (and accurately) identifying and defining any problem, we simultaneously define its solution. Hence, as the problem upon which the vast majority of all other problems besetting our nation are based is the departure from the fundamental or "supreme" law of the land, the *one* – and *only* – solution is to return to that law!.

While some may retort that to do so would be difficult or impossible at this late date, it is nonetheless the *only* way to correct course. There are, in addition, a number of critical steps that *must* be taken in order for us to accomplish this task, and I will delineate them clearly in the pages that follow. Make no mistake, however: we *must* reestablish the *Constitution* as the basis for all of our laws – both extant and future; and doing so will, *without question*, restore both the prosperity and the individual liberties with which we were once blessed, and to which we long to return. I do not offer this as theory, but, rather, as fact. *I have every confidence that WE THE PEOPLE will rise up and make this happen!* The process has already begun, and is clearly visible to all who are *willing* to see!

We *have* the power, and *together* we can and *will* effect the solution!

"THESE are the times that try men's souls. The summer soldier and the sunshine patriot will, in this crisis, shrink from the service of their country; but he that stands by it now, deserves the love and thanks of man and woman. Tyranny, like hell, is not easily conquered; yet we have this consolation with us, that the harder the conflict, the more glorious the triumph. What we obtain too cheap, we esteem too lightly: it is dearness only that gives every thing its value. Heaven knows how to put a proper price upon its goods; and it would be strange indeed if so celestial an article as FREEDOM should not be highly rated. Britain, with an army to enforce her tyranny, has declared that she has a right (not only to TAX) but "to BIND us in ALL CASES WHATSOEVER" and if being bound in that manner, is not slavery, then is there not such a thing as slavery upon earth. Even the expression is impious; for so unlimited a power can belong only to God."

Thomas Paine – *The Crisis* (December 23, 1776)

"I have sworn upon the altar of God, eternal hostility against every form of tyranny over the mind of man."

Thomas Jefferson – Letter to Benjamin Rush, September 23, 1800

In the past, the enemies of liberty have typically operated under the cloak of darkness, never admitting to their true aims, but when the supposed "fourth branch" of government, the "traditional" media, refuses to report or *comment truthfully upon the Congress' or the Administration's obvious abuses of power*, the people look up at the "scoreboard" (of the media) and see that the "score" has not changed (nothing of substance has been recorded).

It is as if *nothing* has happened; thus a large portion of the people (those who are getting their information from the "traditional"/elitist media outlets) are deluded into thinking tha*t nothing has really changed!* Meanwhile, the country they love is being destroyed before their very eyes, and they can't even see it. Those who love party more than truth or country, and see everything through the lens of "us vs. them," are blinded by their own myopic prejudice.

The number of radicals and degree of extremist thought in and around the White House is readily visible to anyone who wants to see and know what is going on. Those who do not are either completely uninformed (they are simply watching the traditional "news" or reading almost any local newspaper, and listening to the "news" on the radio – but not listening to talk radio) or they simply will not see outside of their own traditional viewpoints based on party bias. Fortunately, the majority of the country is at least aware to some degree of what is going on, and a small army – thanks to the *new media* (*Fox News, Talk Radio, Email, YouTube,* and the *Blogosphere*) – is almost *completely* aware of it.

And it is because of that small, but highly informed "army" that those of us with traditional American values will succeed in restoring our country to Constitutio*nal* rule (the *rule of law* - starting with the "Supreme Law of the Land"), which will result in a dramatically reduced government, with greatly reduced taxes and regulations. We will succeed in returning the control of the government to its rightful owners – *THE PEOPLE OF THE UNITED STATES!*

"...no free government, or the blessing of liberty, can be preserved to any people but by a firm adherence to justice, moderation, temperance, frugality, and virtue, and by frequent recurrence to fundamental principles."

George Mason – the *Virginia Declaration of Rights, 1776*

"It does not require a majority to prevail, but rather an irate, tireless minority keen to set brush fires in people's minds."

Samuel Adams

Chapter Eleven

Political Parties and the Debt

In the previous chapter I stated with certainty that we knew the solution to our nation's primary problems. I also indicated that it was simply a matter of re-enshrining the *Constitution* as the *Supreme Law of the Land,* and declared emphatically that it was "the one and only way." My point was that unless we do this, most other measures will be of little effect. Nonetheless, I indicated that "There are, in addition, a number of critical steps that *must* be taken in order for us to accomplish this task...." Let me now give the first of these.

When one is in dire financial straits, burdened with overwhelming debt, there is one absolutely essential step that he or she must take: *He must get rid of his credit cards*. It is the same with an alcoholic or one who is hopelessly addicted to other drugs. Each must remove the means of his downfall. There are, in each of these cases, other steps that must be taken, but one can make no pretense of sincerity without first eliminating the means of his enslavement.

Before stating what I would have assumed would be obvious to every sober observer, I need to put this in perspective. If one includes the unfunded liabilities of Social Security and Medicare, we as a nation may be in debt by more than $210,000,000,000,000 – TWO-HUNDRED AND TEN TRILLION DOLLARS! (http://www.minyanville.com/assets/File/Kotlikoff_USBankruptcy_paper%5B1%5D.pdf).

To put that in perspective, there are roughly 310,000,000 people (three-hundred and ten million) living in the US at present. That means that the individual share for every man, woman, and child in the country is roughly $700,000. Translation: Every person living in America today owes nearly three-quarters of a million dollars – not counting his or her own personal debts. Every one. Do you think we should try to trim off a little here, or a little there...or *do you think it might be time to take bold and decisive action?* What we *don't* need to do is listen to the "experts," *such as the chairman of the House Committee on Financial Services, and the chairman of the Senate Committee on Banking, Housing, and Urban Affairs – Barney Frank and Christopher Dodd respectively.*

It was these two "experts" charged with overseeing the mortgage-loan industry on our behalf, who assured us that lending giants Fannie Mae and Freddie Mac were doing just fine, when in truth the federal mandates to create sub-prime mortgage loans had created a huge housing bubble nationwide, driving the prices of homes through the roof, by flooding the market with loans that people would ultimately be unable to repay. *And you now know how that worked out!*

When people started defaulting on their loans – people who were never qualified to borrow the money in the first place – the bubble burst, bringing on the worst economy "since the Great Depression" – just as the then-presidential candidate who is now our Commander in Chief told us it was...only for the wrong reasons. He blamed it on his predecessor and *his* party, but while there was certainly plenty of blame to go around, the straw that broke the camel's back was the sub-prime loan crisis that resulted from massive defaults – *all policies that he and his party had created and championed!*

So, if you're reading this, you probably recognize that this is no time for timidity. You may recall several months back when hundreds of thousands (or was it millions?) of gallons of oil were allegedly spewing into the Gulf of Mexico every day, and some entity brought in a recovery tanker, ostensibly capable of single-handedly taking on a significant portion of the oil that had spilled into the Gulf up to that point. But no, the environmental experts at the EPA said they needed to delay the action in order to determine the *environmental safety* or *impact* of the tanker and the process!

The economic equivalent of such madness would be to suggest that we "study" the effect that reduced spending would have on the economy. I would find it difficult – if not impossible – to comment on such a position. Only someone entirely incapable of rational thought would suggest such a thing; *only someone completely void of executive experience or the ability to lead would allow it!*

The former White House Chief of Staff has famously quoted this Administration's handbook of operation, *Rules for Radicals*, when he said "Never let a crisis go to waste." He, of course, was speaking of using the crisis for political advantage or gain. What he and the elected head of our government know nothing about is how to actually deal with a crisis – *environmental or economic!*

To suggest that may not be intellectually honest on my part, however. It would, in fact, be difficult to accept that anyone could actually believe that adding trillions of dollars of debt to our already-reeling economy, and trillions of dollars in new entitlement programs, along with over 5,000 pages of bureaucratic rules and regulation, in two new huge pieces of legislation, *would have anything but a devastating effect on the economy!*

Is there anyone reading these words – and they are facts known to all – who believes that a president hailed by many (virtually the entire media establishment) as the most brilliant man to ever occupy the Oval Office, could actually think that the results of these actions would not cripple the economy – to say nothing of our *Constitution* and way of life?

Well, they can't have it both ways. He is either so lacking in common sense that he can't see what the vast majority see without giving it a second thought, or his actions are intentional. He can't be both brilliant and naive. I personally believe he is neither…but his "handling" of the economy is no accident.

In the end, however, it makes little difference. His policies are destroying our nation – economically and constitutionally. He did say, after all, that he intended to "fundamentally transform…America." But I digress….The broader point I wish to make is that in facing a real (not manufactured) crisis, *we must take bold and decisive action. This is no time for timidity or a lack of vision or courage!*

Once again, before pointing out a solution so obvious that it should be on the lips of every conservative "leader" in the country, I must once again point out the sad truth. *That truth is that we have people in both political parties who are more interested in their own lifestyles than those of the people who hired them and pay their not-insignificant salaries, and exorbitant retirement benefits!*

It has seemed to me as a careful observer that those pretending to be "conservative" speak one way to conservative audiences, and another way to their "colleagues" in the House or Senate where they are allegedly to do "THE PEOPLE'S" business. They are ardently *partisan*, though *it can be readily seen that their party is merely a convenience!*

We have seen this abundantly as more than one national figure has switched parties in recent years after losing in the primaries. (Several have also further disgraced themselves by refusing to call and congratulate the true conservatives whom THE PEOPLE have chosen to replace them!)

One of these announced today that she will be running as a write-in candidate – with the potential of damaging her more conservative victor from the primary, by splitting the "Independent" vote. Such conduct from one who pretended for years to "represent the people" of her state, and to stand on principle, speaks volumes about her true "ideology" (http://homernews.com/stories/100610/news_mfi.shtml).

Clearly, these "establishment Republicans" have one objective, and that is to stay in power! Well, the people of the country are disgusted with their overt self-centeredness, and *we feel no allegiance to parties!*

We are committed to *principles!* Yes, most of us have voted Republican for most of our lives, but only because the Republicans were supposed to believe in smaller constitutional government, less spending, less regulation, and less taxation.

Here is a bulletin to the parties, the pollsters, and the media elites: The majority of people currently registered as *Independents* are not "moderates." We are both passionate conservatives and "regular" people who love our country – hard-working citizens who care nothing for parties! We are the true main stream of America, and we are neither "centrist" nor "undecided!"

The only ones who believe – *or want us and others to believe* – that we are "on the fringe" are those who are themselves completely outside of the mainstream. The idea that either Hollywood or the elite media represent the views of average Americans is laughable!

Not only do they not share the views of most Americans, they consider both those views and those of us who hold them as antiquated and out of step. Without question they share the current President's view as a "citizen of the world," rather than that held by the vast majority of us *who humbly and gratefully acknowledge American exceptionalism!*

The elite media were able to disguise the truth in the past, when they were the only available source of information. Now that we have Talk Radio, the Internet, and Fox News, the one-time monopoly has been broken. And as commentator Glenn Beck has repeatedly observed, "the truth will make [us] free." In this case, it *has* made us free – and it is about to make us freer than we have been for the past 50-100 years!

I will also credit "Brother Beck" with the understanding that the first time a depression was successfully avoided in the last century was under Warren G. Harding in 1920. He did it by slashing both taxes and government spending. The result was that a depression was avoided and the recession ended in some eighteen months. What happened next was what we now know as *The Roaring Twenties* – a decade of unprecedented prosperity.

There are, of course, Republicans who are not the least bit conservative. Already seven Republican Senators have lost to more conservative candidates in their primaries in the past few months. Perhaps the most disturbing result – *to those who are not truly conservative* – just took place in Delaware. In a not-so-surprising aftermath, a number of prominent national Republicans – both before *and* after the Primary, as it turns out – attacked the more inexperienced "Tea Party" candidate!

Meanwhile, just a few days ago, the Republican "leadership" released their "Pledge." *It is a step that needed to be taken*, and it appears to contain several good ideas, such as requiring all proposed legislation to reference chapter and verse of Constitutional authority. That is spot on, but may not go far enough. We'll see. (I've been too busy writing to stop and read it all yet!) *My assumption, however – and I'd be willing to wager a large sum on this if I were a 'betting man' – is that because the document was written by 'insiders,' it lacks boldness!*

There is one recommendation, however, that is completely counter to what we must do to save our economy and our individual freedoms. That recommendation is *to return to 2008 spending levels!* This is the very picture of timidity! According to *Wikipedia*, "The U.S. Federal Government collected $2.52 trillion in FY [Fiscal Year] 2008, while budgeted spending was $2.98 trillion, generating a total deficit of $455 billion." *The deficit this very year was roughly three times that!*

So, we are in a true economic crisis, the economy is collapsing, unemployment has been *reported* at an alleged 9.6% for months, we are drowning in debt, and the Republican establishment is recommending that we *"cut back"* to a *half-trillion dollar annual deficit?!*

The good things in their *"Pledge"* notwithstanding, *this is not leadership!* This is near *paralysis!* What we need – *and we've needed it for a long time!* – is a Balanced Budget Amendment!

We must take away the government credit card! We can argue at length over what is a legitimate (constitutionally authorized) government expense – and we will for as long as it takes to restore the *Constitution* to its rightful place – but in the meantime, we must simply *defund* the federal government. (Without question, this should be done on every state and local level as well.) *Yes*, we take away the credit card! *We* are the parents...*not the other way around!*

Oh, *"but that could never pass!"* Really? Would *you* be in favor of it? Do you know anyone whom you respect who wouldn't be in favor of it? Well, my friend, the time for our "representatives" to tell *us* what will or will not pass has indeed *passed!* We have witnessed over the past two years a government and its "representatives" who have both ignored and openly defied the American people, and we have decided that we will no longer allow it. That day is over!

So it is time for us to stop saying – or even *thinking!* – that that which we want, or don't want, "could never pass." If we want it, we needn't settle for anything less! WE, THE PEOPLE, have been awakened, and we intend to have the "liberty and justice for all" that we were promised in the *original Pledge!*

I ask you: What form of government do we have if it is not a government "of the people, by the people, for the people"? I will answer that we have whatever form of government we are willing to accept, but it is nothing short of tyranny! Those whom we elect to represent us *briefly*, will either do so, or we will dismiss them. *They work for us!* The only way that they can remain in our "service" is for us, their employers, to allow it, and we are no longer willing to tolerate those whom we hire and pay, defying us! *We* are *their* masters! (We will discuss term limits shortly!)

"I am committed against every thing which, in my judgment, may weaken, endanger, or destroy [the Constitution]...and especially against all extension of Executive power; any attempt to rule the free people of this country with the power and the patronage of the Government itself...."

Daniel Webster – Works of Daniel Webster, Volume I – 1851 (p. 336)

"The spirit of resistance to government is so valuable on certain occasions, that I wish it always to be kept alive."

> Thomas Jefferson

"In questions of power, then, let no more be heard of confidence in man, but bind him down from mischief by the chains of the Constitution."
> Thomas Jefferson

The "party" is over!

Chapter Twelve

The "Plenary Power" to Tax

Years ago I was writing a book about the "Tennessee Tax Revolt." A Republican Governor who had run twice on a promise of no state income tax had attempted to instigate one against the will of the majority of the people of the state – and we would not (and ultimately *did not*) allow it. I will not go into the story here, but while reviewing State Supreme Court cases, I came across the phrase "the plenary power of the state to tax" the citizens.

Not being familiar with the term, I looked it up. What it means is: "complete in every respect: absolute, unqualified" (Merriam-Webster Dictionary). I can only tell you that I was stunned! The *plenary power to tax?* I couldn't believe it! *What arrogant judge, or group of judges thought the government had the "absolute" power to tax anything that they felt the need or the desire to tax?*

I will tell you that I was then, and am now *outraged* at the very thought of it! Apparently these "legal scholars" had not the least understanding of the foundational principle upon which any legitimate government rests. That being that the only legitimate authority that any government has is that which is granted to it by its rightful sovereigns, THE PEOPLE!

It was clear to me then, and remains so now, that the power to tax is *the power to destroy!* It is the power to seize property, and we should grant no government that power, *without first proscribing the very limited duties with which it is tasked.* I must, however, say that we as a people have long since relinquished ownership of our government....Now it is time for us to take it back – *and we started that process on November 2, 2010!*

"We the People are the rightful masters of both Congress and the Courts--not to overthrow the Constitution, but to overthrow the men who pervert the Constitution."

Abraham Lincoln

http://cancertutor.com/Quotes/Quotes_Presidents.html

"It is sufficiently obvious, that persons and property are the two great subjects on which Governments are to act; and that the rights of persons, and the rights of property, are the objects, for the protection of which Government was instituted. These rights cannot be separated."

James Madison - *Speech at the Virginia Convention, December 2, 1829*

"It is the duty of the patriot to protect his country from its government."
Thomas Paine

"The probability that we may fall in the struggle ought not to deter us from the support of a cause we believe to be just; it shall not deter me. If ever I feel the soul within me elevate and expand to those dimensions not wholly unworthy of its almighty Architect, it is when I contemplate the cause of my country deserted by all the world beside, and I standing up boldly and alone, and hurling defiance at her victorious oppressors. Here, without contemplating consequences, before high heaven and in the face of the world, I swear eternal fidelity to the just cause, as I deem it, of the land of my life, my liberty, and my love."

President Abraham Lincoln, *Speech, Springfield, Illinois, Dec 20, 1839*. I, 137, in Archer H. Shaw, *The Lincoln Encyclopedia* (New York: Macmillan, 1950), p. 64. Full quote from *Project Gutenberg*

I think it is clear that it is the duty that we owe to our children and our posterity to take hold once more of the reins of government. Can we think of the great men who went before us and not follow their lead?

I must point out that while some (even at least one "financial" reporter from the Wall Street Journal) have not grasped that lowering tax rates increases tax revenues, it is simply a fact. During the Reagan Era, average tax rates were reduced by half, and the tax revenues doubled.

So, while those who do not grasp this simple fact would immediately say that not allowing the government to borrow must necessarily mean that we will have to raise taxes. Not so. *Not only will we not raise taxes, we will dramatically reduce them!*

When I stated that we needed to take the credit card away from the government, I wasn't just suggesting that we should stop borrowing (stop deficit spending immediately), I was stating that we must dramatically reduce government spending *across the board!*

So, just as Warren G. Harding, and later his vice president Calvin Coolidge, did in 1920, we must slash both spending and taxes; *and returning to a half-trillion dollar deficit is not "slashing" spending!* To suggest that as "fiscal responsibility" is to either not understand the severity of our current economic malaise, or to simply lack the courage to confront it!

I have no doubt that the difficulty with this arises from the politicians knowing how many entitlements and other expenditures there are, and being concerned with the "political" ramifications. Well, when they are being sent to Washington for one or two terms max, and we are sending them for the exclusive purpose of dramatically reducing the size, scope, and *expense* of government, they won't be so concerned with garnering votes from special interests!

As was the case during the *Gingrich Revolution*, and the *Contract With America,* the establishment media will condemn every last cut, but they will simply continue to marginalize themselves...if they continue to exist at all! My point is that they are irrelevant! They speak only for themselves and their own ideology – not for the bulk of America – *so we should simply pay them no heed!*

"The greatest [calamity] which could befall [us would be] submission to a government of unlimited powers."

Thomas Jefferson, *Declaration and Protest of Virginia, 1825. The Writings of Thomas Jefferson,*(Memorial Edition) Lipscomb and Bergh, editors, ME 17:445

Chapter Thirteen

"All You Need to Know"

And now I wish to point out how certain simple observations can often tell us *all we need to know* about a given subject. For instance, I have never done an exhaustive study of communism. I have read a number of books by Ayn Rand, who left Russia in the early 1920's, I believe, shortly after the Bolshevik "Revolution." She lived under communism long enough, however, to write *We The Living,* in which she described in great detail what life was like in the new "workers' paradise." *It was Hell!*

In addition to the knowledge I have gained from reading, however, I often remember an insightful observation made about Russia and the United States, which summed up the two systems – communism and capitalism – or free enterprise. It is simply this: Communist countries build walls and fences to keep people in; we, on the other hand, build fences to keep people out (*figuratively,* at least!). That is it. One could easily – and *accurately* – judge the two systems based on that single observation.

Similarly, some on the Left have praised Castro's Cuban health care system, and even called it superior to our own. Meanwhile, I have observed one thing: To my knowledge, no American has ever tried to "escape" to Cuba from the US in a small water craft. (The very idea, of course, seems preposterous! What need would one have to "escape" from America?)

On the other hand, countless numbers of Cubans have risked their lives in the shark-infested waters that separate our two countries, by doing just that! Some, of course, have lost their lives in making the attempt.

In addition, the vast majority of those Cubans who come here become Republicans (Senator-elect Marco Rubio of Florida), not Democrats. They do that because they appreciate the opportunity and freedom that America offers, and they have seen the evils of total state control. Those two observations alone should come close to telling everything that needs to be known about communism or nationalized health care. Of course one or the other could be great, but apparently the combination isn't! (And, frankly, *didn't you already know "all you need[ed] to know" about Cuba anyway?*)

A third example in the all-you-need-to-know category is the fact that so many Canadians – including the head of their national health care system who has banned private medical practice even for those who wish to pay their own way – along with Middle Eastern Oil Sheiks and everyone else in the world who can afford it (including the late lion of *one-size-fits-all health care*, Ted Kennedy) come to the US for the finest specialized treatments money can buy. (Meanwhile, it isn't *"fair"* that some can afford these things while others cannot – unless, of course, "some" happen to be public "servants," with their own government "plan" – they, of course, deserve something better!)

And since the elite media, now nothing more than a *pep squad for progressives*, is almost certainly the most dishonest "broker" in the entire "transformation of America," I must add one more "small" example from an article on today's *CNN* website – the self-proclaimed "most trusted name in news" (http://www.cnn.com/2010/US/09/29/okeefe.cnn.prank/index.html?eref=mrss_igoogle_cnn).

The article about James O'Keefe, *"best known for hitting the community organizing group ACORN with an undercover video sting"* seeks, with what appears to be a fair amount of validity, to disparage O'Keefe. In doing so, however, it displays not just bias on behalf of the highly questionable, if not fully discredited, organization, *ACORN*, a key supporter and long-time partner of our current president, but a clear unwillingness to be open and state key facts, all the while seeking to make *ACORN* appear to be a noble organization which was simply an innocent victim. (See if you can pick out the key words and phrases that tell you "all you need to know.")

"O'Keefe is best known for making a series of undercover videos inside ACORN offices around the country in 2009. The 40-year-old liberal group was crippled by scandal after O'Keefe and fellow activist Hannah Giles allegedly solicited advice from ACORN workers on setting up a brothel and evading taxes."

The videos led to some of the employees being fired and contributed to the disbanding of ACORN, which advocated for low- and middle-income and worked to register voters."

So, this *"40-year-old"* (substitute "well established," "venerable," or "respectable") *"liberal group"* (i.e., only targeted by the Right because it is on the Left – *not* because it was already charged with voter registration fraud in half a dozen states or more, while receiving *BILLIONS of dollars in taxpayer money*) was "crippled by scandal" *only* "after O'Keefe" and others "allegedly" sought advice from *ACORN* employees on *"setting up a brothel and evading taxes."*

Note that they were only *"crippled by scandal after O'Keefe"* performed his sting – even though the multiple indictments were outstanding *before* he targeted them, and were the reason he did so.

Perhaps my favorite euphemistic term is *"alleged."* While *CNN* is no court of law, it pretends that it must not "convict" the defendant "before the trial." In fact, tens of millions of Americans no doubt saw the videos (on *Fox News* and *YouTube*) in which O'Keefe and his female companion *clearly* – not *"allegedly"* – sought and received advice from *ACORN* officials, for the stated purpose of not simply setting up a brothel in public housing (while evading taxes) but for doing so with some thirteen under-aged girls from El Salvador.

While brothels might be "socially acceptable" in some circles, hopefully, prostitution rings using enslaved under-aged girls are not. They most definitely are not for those in the *real* mainstream of America!

Finally, *CNN* dutifully informs us that *ACORN* is nothing more than an "advocacy group" for the *"low- and middle-income (sic) [people?]"* which *"worked to register voters."* As noted, however, they glaringly fail to mention that they, *ACORN*, had already been indicted by numerous states and municipalities on charges of voter-registration fraud, *along with the hugely important facts that they are closely tied to the president, and have received – and are still receiving,* in spite of a temporary halt as a result of the sting – *billions of dollars of taxpayer money.*

You will have to decide whether the writer of the article (and the editing partner at *CNN*) were simply not very thorough, or careful, in their "reporting," or whether these glaring omissions were *by design*.

Given that I consider myself to be of "average" intelligence, I graciously attribute the same to *CNN*, and can only assume, therefore, that the "oversights" were no accident – which, in a word, makes them deliberate "prevarications."

Even in an article (entitled *CNN Fails to Stop Fall in Ratings*, March 29, 2010) by head cheer leader, *The New York Times,* which "covers" *CNN's* "*precipitous decline in ratings*" (their words), while acknowledging *Fox News'* continued unprecedented growth rates (25-50% in various programs) – even after its best year ever in 2009 – the "newspaper of record" fails to give a bottom-line statistic comparing *CNN's* vs. *Fox's* total viewership. (This would be akin to reporting on a sporting event and not bothering to give the final score. Am I the only one who would expect to hear what that is without having to go look it up? *I think not!*)

In addition, the article states the following – without making the obviously-called-for remark on its absurdity:

"CNN executives have steadfastly said that they will not change their approach to prime-time programs, which are led by hosts not aligned with any partisan point of view." [Please!]

To make sure that there is no misunderstanding on this point, it is a simple fact that to the elites in the 'ruling class,' to be "liberal" is to be *unbiased*, while being "conservative" is to be not only *biased*, but "*extremist*" or "*radical*" as well!

One can state openly, and on the record, that *"Any health care funding plan that is just, equitable, civilized, and humane must, must redistribute wealth from the richer among us to the poorer and the less fortunate"* and, that *"Excellent health care is by definition redistributional."** as the new Medicare Czar, Donald Berwick, has done; or, be an openly avowed revolutionary communist,** such as Van Jones, former "Green Jobs" Czar, both appointed by the current president of the United States, and *CNN* not only avoids calling *them* – or their positions – *radical,* but fails to cover them at all (giving undeniable "cover" to both them and this Administration)!

*http://www.prisonplanet.com/obamas-new-health-care-czar-we-must-redistribute-wealth.html
**http://www.examiner.com/conservative-politics-in-national/van-jones-green-jobs-czar-a-self-described-communist-arrested-during-rodney-king-riots

In a "shocking" new development, now that *CNN's* ratings are somewhere between a third and a fourth those of *Fox*, their President, Jonathan Klein, was just given his *one-day* notice. In an article on a *CBS* affiliate website, the *CNN* magic was explained by observing that *"its non-partisan stance makes it bland"* (http://www.bnet.com/blog/new-media/with-jonathan-klein-dismissal-cnn-finally-pushes-the-panic-button/6204).

My point in all of this *CNN* commentary is simply to illustrate that if the elite media (and *CNN* is front and center in that consortium) will blatantly misrepresent the facts in a single, but important, news article, how much more does one need to know about them or their cohorts? Notice that in the two other sources (*NY Times* and *CBS*) commenting on *CNN,* both completely supported the notion that *CNN* was "non-partisan" or unbiased!

I must acknowledge that *CNN* did break an *ACORN* voter-fraud story in Lake County, Indiana, on October 10, 2008, which appeared to be quite "fair and balanced," and even pointed out that then-presidential-candidate Barack Obama had represented *ACORN* in the past(http://hillbuzz.org/2008/10/13/cnn-exposes-obamaacorn-voter-fraud-in-indiana/).

However, I was unable to find a single follow-up report on the obviously important question concerning the relationship between a major presidential candidate (who would shortly thereafter become president, and thus further underscore the seriousness of the question) and a group that was mired in allegations of voter-registration fraud, throughout the nation – even though there has since been another widely circulated video (released on Thursday, 18 February, 2010, by Representative Darrell Issa [R-CA], ranking member on the House Committee on Oversight and Government Reform) in which the now-president stated the following:

Before reading the quote, you may wish to *Google* "Darrel Issa CBS ABC NBC 18 February 2010" and see if you come up with any "breaking news" on this matter. To save you the trouble, here it is

(http://www.google.com/search?q=18+February%2C+2010%2C+by+Representative+Darrell+Issa+cnn%2Cabc%2Cnbc%2Ccbs+&rls=com.microsoft:*:IE-SearchBox&ie=UTF-8&oe=UTF-8&sourceid=ie7&rlz=1I7ADBR_en):

What you *will find* are numerous stories about how *none of the networks covered the story*. (You may also enjoy a number of other related items on another site I came across while looking into this:

http://conservativeamerican.org/obama-administration-scandals-list/page-23-1101-1200/).

Now for the damning (in most universes, at least) quote:

"When I ran project vote, the voter registration drive in Illinois, ACORN was smack dab in the middle of it. Once I was elected there wasn't a campaign that ACORN worked on down in Springfield that I wasn't right there with you. Since I have been in the United States Senate I've been always a partner with ACORN as well. I've been fighting with ACORN, along side ACORN, on issues you care about my entire career."

The release of the video came *after* he "clarified" his relationship with *ACORN for a reporter* in the following interview, in October, 2008 – just prior to the election (http://gatewaypundit.firstthings.com/2010/02/oh-me-oh-my-obama-caught-in-a-major-acorn-lie-video/):

Reporter: *"Senator McCain today said there was voter fraud going on in the battleground states. ACORN has been tampering with America's most precious right. There has to be a full investigation and he also said you need to disclose your full relationship with ACORN. I'm wondering if you have any reaction to Senator McCain's charge?"*

Barack Obama: *"Well, first of all my relationship with ACORN is pretty straightforward. It's probably 13 years ago when I was still practicing law, I represented ACORN and my partner in that investigation was the US Justice department in having Illinois implement what was called the motor voter law, to make sure people could go to DMV's and driver license facilities to get registered. It wasn't being implemented. That was my relationship and is my relationship to ACORN. There is an ACORN organization in Chicago. They've been active. As an elected official, I've had interactions with them. But, they're not advising my campaign. We've got the best voter registration in politics right now and we don't need ACORN's help."* Right!

So, here we have the President of the United States caught lying on video tape about his relationship with an organization involved in massive voter-registration fraud, and while *CNN* was instrumental in breaking the original story, they apparently had no interest in investigating or following up on the matter – even after a House Oversight Committee released its own tremendously damning follow-up.

I don't know of any other way to frame this. At best, it is professional incompetence on an alarming scale (not a single individual in an entire network of "journalists," "reporters," and "news editors" found the revelation noteworthy), *or* it is a violation of professional ethics of the worst kind. It is the responsibility of *every* – but especially the *major* – "news" organizations, in a "free" society, to inform the populace of issues regarding their safety and their liberty.

To fail to report a deep and long-held tie between a sitting president (*"I've been fighting...along side ACORN, on issues [they] care about my entire career."*) and an organization not only under investigation for years over extensive fraudulent activities involving the sanctity of the voting process, but which is also the beneficiary of massive taxpayer funding while openly advocating for a particular political party, *is a gross violation of the public trust!*

I hasten to add, in conclusion, that with the exception of *Fox News* no other major "news" network, that I could find, covered the latter (damning) revelation. While this is only one example in an endless string of similar abuses across all of the liberal media outlets, it should serve as sufficient evidence, to all thinking persons, that they cannot be trusted!

How could one *rationally* assume that any organization (whose responsibility it is to bring truth to the public) knowingly "spins" (or simply covers up by failing to report) an important story, would not do the same relative to any story with which it did not agree in the future? *He or she could not!* The only *rational conclusion* is that it would do exactly that – *and that unquestioningly appears to be the record!*

The elite media, which purports to be an unbiased reporter of the facts, has, in reality, an undeniable paradigm or world view, and today it is on full display for all to see, as never before. For them to pretend otherwise (as they still do) while denouncing anyone who dares to suggest even *bias*, only underscores their complete disconnect with the regular "folks" (Bill O'Reilly).

Meanwhile, both the old-guard media and the current Administration and its party's leaders have openly denounced and attacked the one news organization that is worthy of the name: *Fox News.* Yes, they lean Right (as do most of their show hosts) – in contrast to all of their faltering "competitors" – but that makes them the *only* major outlet where one can actually hear more than an occasional token spokesperson for the Right...and apparently (if ratings mean anything), the true *mainstream* of America, are in favor!

So, is *CNN* really *"The Most Trusted Name in News!"* as it claims to be? They (obviously) would have you think so...*but* (since ratings tell us "all we need to know") *apparently you don't!*

Chapter Fourteen

Conventional "Wisdom"

Liberals or "Progressives" (a term historically used by those who sympathized with Marxists and Communists) only win elections by pretending to be "moderate," and hiding their true beliefs and intentions. Conservatives, on the other hand, often lose precisely because they fail to identify their true motives. The "conventional *wisdom*" that conservatives are not "electable" in "moderate" or "liberal" states or jurisdictions is absurd, as well as cowardly!

Our last "unelectable" president was Ronald Reagan! When we have to either hide or abandon our principles to be elected, then we truly deceive ourselves – as well as those whom we seek to influence. As Jim Demint, apparently the most conservative *leader* in the *US Senate*, recently put it: "I don't want to be part of a majority that doesn't stand for anything." He was and *is* exactly right!

Conventional "wisdom" says that you must first win in order to have influence or power. The false premise that accompanies that assumption is that in order to win a true conservative must disguise his bedrock principles and beliefs. *That, in fact, would be to bear false witness!* We simply need to be honest. There *may* be times when overt honesty would be unwise – such as in the *Old Testament* account of Abraham introducing his reportedly beautiful wife Sarah as his "sister," in order to save his life – but those times are few and far between...and, for the record, Sarah *was* Abraham's half-sister.

I sincerely believe the old adage that *"Honesty is the best policy!"* When we tell the truth – even when doing so puts us at risk – *people soon know that we can be trusted.* Imagine the difference between knowing that a president or other elected official would *never lie or misrepresent the truth,* compared to knowing from repeated experience that he would say whatever he needed to say to advance his own purposes. *That is precisely where we stand today!* Some months back when a certain member of Congress yelled out *"You lie!"* during a nationally televised speech, *that may well have been the only true statement made the entire night* – and he was officially reprimanded (even by some in his own party) for making it! (While some will mock this assertion, I challenge them to go back and fact check every statement made in the speech that night...*then* we'll talk!)

Yes, I believe in decorum, but there are times when one is compelled to speak out, no matter how unpopular his truth. True men and women always respond favorably to such courage and integrity. It is time that we all start speaking the truth, rather than carefully weighing what others – including the media – might say or think. Those who love truth will salute (and follow) us, while those who do not will always attack our conservative positions. The only way to be "loved" by the elitist media is to not stand up for the truth...so why would we pay them heed? *They can only determine the outcome of the debate in this day of New Media if we allow them to influence us!* Any conservative who does not get this will be incapable of leading!

It is, of course, true that in this age of "sound bites," both politicians and their media cohorts will seize upon any verbal misstep and use it against those whom they seek to discredit or destroy. This practice, while justified by its adherents as being "necessary" to promote their presumed pious end, is, in the end, *the very opposite of piety!*

An example from the historical record will suffice to make my point. During his campaign against the incumbent president, Ronald Reagan apparently made reference to the depressed economy. Immediately, the old-guard media leapt into action and confronted Mr. Reagan over the comment. They took exception to his using the term "depression."

Perhaps having had time to give the matter some thought, when asked, he calmly responded with his now-classic explanation: *"[A] Recession is when your neighbor loses his job. [A] Depression is when you lose yours. And a recovery is when [the current occupant of the White House] loses his."*

President Reagan (he won in an historic landslide) could have played it safe and not spoken so plainly in the first place, but he simply spoke what he perceived to be the truth. Perhaps the only greater line in his two terms as president was the one he employed in a speech at the Brandenburg Gate in Berlin:

"General Secretary Gorbachev, if you seek peace, if you seek prosperity for the Soviet Union and Eastern Europe, if you seek liberalization: Come here to this gate! Mr. Gorbachev, open this gate! Mr. Gorbachev, tear down this wall!"

True leaders have little patience with those who wish to play it safe!

Reportedly, a number of his closest advisors had warned him against using such "harsh" (blatantly *true*) language, but he refused to succumb, and chose, instead, to be forthright. That speech – and I would pinpoint it to *that line* – is credited by some with marking *"the beginning of the end of the Cold War and the fall of communism"* (http://usgovinfo.about.com/od/historicdocuments/a/teardownwall.htm).

Like President Reagan, *we too have the power!* So let us stand for truth, and say exactly what it is that we believe, and exactly what we plan to do with those beliefs!

We must also not engage in sugar-coating the truth. In trying to make a tax that the true extremists (those in government) are considering, sound like something that it is not, both its proponents and its media chorus have labeled it a "Value-Added Tax" or *VAT*. That is the height of insult. What is worse, however, is when those on the side of smaller government also employ such patently dishonest euphemisms. Does *anyone* actually believe that *any* tax adds value to either themselves or to the products they are purchasing? Political Correctness has almost no place on the side of truth!

The same must be said for "our side" acquiescing to use such terms as "pro-choice" – when the entire effect of *Roe v. Wade* was to immediately take choice away from the states and the citizens of each state – not to mention the millions of babies (*not* mere *"fetuses"*) whose lives are taken through the heinous practice of abortion. The vast majority of abortions are no doubt the result of voluntary *choices* that people make – often, in the case of those not married, to engage in immoral acts. *The time to "choose" is before taking the initial step which results in the creation of a life!*

As is usually the case, one misdeed or sin usually leads to another. So, in many instances, one starts with a decision or choice to commit an immoral act, and that is followed by the even more immoral act of ending, or *taking*, the life that has started to grow and develop in the womb. Not inconsistently, those who are in favor of – or, at the very least, supportive of – this entire sequence, then engage in the final sin and deception of seeking to justify the whole process by calling it something that it clearly is not: "pro choice." It is simply a mischaracterization of the truth, and none of us should dignify this tragic sequence of sin by spinning it as such. Both a rose and a thorn *"by any other name"* are still a rose or a thorn!

It's also mind-numbing how the *pro-abortion* argument is additionally framed in terms of "a woman's right to control her own body," and yet its same proponents are totally enamored with the idea of countless bureaucrats deciding who will get what treatments for their bodies!

They say, for now, that rationing will not exist (though even in the midst of the debate, mammogram screenings, highly recommended for women in their forties, were cut from *Medicare* for women under 50 in the Health Care bill) – and that costs won't go up for anyone (except "the rich," no doubt) – *but it would be impossible for any rational being to accept such ludicrous propositions!*
(Mammogram screening reference:
http://www.boston.com/news/nation/washington/articles/2009/12/04/senate_passes_coverage_for_mammograms_cuts_in_medicare/.)

One wonders how long it will be until the Congress decides to 'legislate against the law of gravity'...until one realizes with some surprise that stepping in to prevent companies, *or entire segments of the economy*, from failing...*or falling*, is precisely that – *legislating against gravity!*

While those who concocted the income tax were simply seeking an endless source of revenue from which to fund their every plan and program, the government has no business whatsoever knowing our personal incomes. The Left valiantly defends the "right of privacy," and yet they ardently favor – while taking every conceivable deduction – confiscatory (dreamily called *"progressive"*) rates of taxation...all based upon declaring not only one's income, but every detail of how they spent what they earned or otherwise received!

Those who seek to rule us believe that it is their right to not only know our incomes and expenditures – how offensive is it to think about having to justify all of these details of our private lives to the government whose sole responsibility (and authority – *granted by us*) is to protect our personal liberties – but to confiscate whatever portion they deem necessary for the "greater good." In truth, of course, they care little for the *"greater good."* (The father of our current president believed that it was the government's "right" to take 100% of income so long as everyone had food, clothing, shelter, and – one assumes – "health care." See the book, *The Roots of Obama's Rage*, by Dinesh D'Souza.)

The IRS code has now grown to over 75,000 pages – an estimated 65,000,000 words (at 850 words per page). The Lords law of tithing (10%) is found in Malachi 3:10 – "Bring ye all the tithes into the storehouse..." – *eight words!* I know of at least one church which operates primarily from a voluntary tithe, which is probably paid in full by only a third of its members – a "guesstimate" on my part.

This church has for decades completed, on average, one new church building per day, every day of the year, and pays cash for each one. It is also self-insured. It does not insure any of its buildings, because it is cheaper to simply pay for whatever damages might occur to one of its buildings than to insure each one.

Interestingly, this same church is often criticized for its massive wealth – and all of that from a 10% voluntary contribution on gross incomes, from an estimated (on my part) third of its members (an average contribution of 3 1/3 % per member, if my assumption is correct). For the record, this church also operates the largest privately-owned welfare system in the world, and has for decades. It operates three major universities, and is entirely debt free – and, to my knowledge, receives no money from the federal government.

When we see something like the Health Care Bill (2,500 pages?) or the Financial Reform Bill (2,700 pages?), or the IRS Code (75,000+) pages, and you realize that at least two of these, are only "outlines" of the regulatory structure, which will ultimately lead to many thousands of additional pages detailing the voluminous regulations, you can be fairly certain that all of this is an egregious violation of the specific powers enumerated in the *Constitution (in fewer than 10 standard-sized – not legal-sized – pages, including all 27 Amendments!).*

I, for one, recommend the Lord's plan: *"Bring ye all the tithes into the storehouse...that there might be meat in mine house"* (Malachi 3:10 – *Eight words to state what was required...and eight more to explain why!).*

"Simplicity is the ultimate sophistication."

Leonardo DaVinci

Chapter Fifteen

The *Call to Arms!*

Enough said. I will now conclude by offering the basic steps that I believe we must take to save our nation. You will notice immediately that these are not mere platitudes. When I see so-called conservatives now running on platforms of merely "reducing spending, and lowering taxes" I realize that while their hearts and their values may be in the right place, they are not leaders. When the nation is drowning in debt, taxation, and regulation, it is not time to "play it safe" politically! *If any aspiring conservative representative isn't going to Washington to make dramatic changes, then he or she should simply stay home!* In recent years – and, frankly, for most of our lives – the Republicans have simply been *Socialist 'Lite!'* The point is, that their policies have lead just as surely to massive government bureaucracy and intrusion into our wallets and our lives! In most cases, they have just been a little slower in getting there. The end, however, has been the same – and we have now nearly arrived at the final, gray, state-controlled *paradise* (*protected from life and all of its potential pit falls...as well as its joys!*) Here is my solution:

1. Enact a Federal Balanced Budget Amendment.

As a result of the Woodrow Wilson Administration and its expansive policies, both prior to and as a result of World War I, in 1920 the national economy was near 'melt-down.' The top personal income tax rate had risen to an astonishing 77 percent (after starting at 6% just four years earlier), and the country was "deeply in debt." In precisely the same way that it is doing today, the newly-created *Fed* (*Federal Reserve*) lowered interest rates and began to print money.

In fact, the whole picture was nearly identical to the state in which we find ourselves today – in terms of both an ever-expanding, and increasingly-more-intrusive government, and an economy in its death throes. (Unlike then, however, while we too find ourselves with extremely low interest rates, the banks which we bailed out with taxpayer money are not willing to make loans. The larger banks that received the money, used it to buy up smaller banks, and made themselves that much bigger and wealthier. *Now* if they fail, there will be an even greater devastating effect on the economy as a whole.)

According to Thomas E. Woods, author of *Meltdown*, in an interview on the Glenn Beck program on Tax Day (April 15th) of 2010:

"Between 1920 and '22, the federal budget was, in fact, cut roughly in half. They cut top marginal income tax rates and marginal income tax rates for all groups substantially throughout the '20s. After they cut marginal tax rates so substantially, they were also able to cut the national debt, not the deficit, the national debt by one-third during the 1920s."

Beck responded by reiterating:

"The budget was cut in half. Tax rates reduced in all income brackets. The national debt reduced by one-third. In 18 months, America rebounded. The result: the "Roaring '20s....Limited government and free enterprise fueled one of the greatest success stories in American history."

Woods continued: "We never hear a thing about the depression of 1920, for obvious reasons, because we might draw the wrong conclusions. We might conclude that maybe these policies could be implemented today....So, this episode is simply left off the table."

Beck concluded by pointing out that after eight years of greatly reduced government spending and taxation – and the resulting prosperity – under presidents Harding and Calvin Coolidge, president Herbert Hoover *"following Woodrow Wilson's progressive playbook of bloated government, massive spending and sky-high taxes led us back to the brink, the Great Depression."*

"In another undeniable example of progressive revisionist history, [we] have all been taught that FDR's New Deal proved to be the salvation of America. Nothing could be further from the truth. The New Deal expanded government to levels approaching a dictatorship. Taxes reached obscene levels and the era of government entitlements, many of which are still choking our economy today, was born. The New Deal prolonged the Great Depression in America. As other countries around the world rebounded years earlier, America suffered through a full decade of hardship."

This stunning "lesson" from history concludes with the FDR "playbook" serving *as the model for our leaders today as America, once again, suffers through a crisis brought on by progressive leadership* (http://www.foxnews.com/story/0,2933,590865,00.html).

The first thing we must do is to stop the borrowing! *This can be made permanent through a Balanced Budget Amendment!*

2. Abolish the *Income Tax* and the *IRS.* Replace both with a single *National Sales Tax*.

What I am proposing is a sales tax at the point of sale for all goods sold; *no deductions, no exceptions, no forms to fill out or file.* No IRS, no tax accountants, no tax lawyers. *No waste of time or energy either planning around, or calculating the taxes due.* No bureaucracy to decide which products or industries are to be exempted, with which formulae or rate; just an electronic deduction at the point of sale, which is directly transferred into the government bank account with nothing but technical experts to make sure that the electronic transfers continue to work as installed. No receipts to keep – other than for one's own personal or business records. No need to justify anything to the government. *You make a purchase, the tax is deducted on the spot, and you have nothing to prove, file – or hide.*

One economist, Art Laffer, a member of Ronald Reagan's Economic Policy Advisory Board, has calculated that an 11% Personal Income Tax and an 11% tax on all business "net sales" would cover "Capital gains, estate tax, FICA, Medicare, [and] Medicaid" – *all* federal taxes apparently. On the same Glenn Beck show quoted from above, Laffer stated that *"we would match the total revenues we collect today with no Laffer Curve at that"* (http://www.foxnews.com/story/0,2933,590865,00.html).

Interestingly, while looking this up I came across a headline that read *"Laffer Curve Discredited".* I found that amusing because, to my knowledge, the *Laffer Curve* does not purport to be a scientific measurement at all, but rather a theoretical construct – *the obvious truth of which can hardly be disputed.*

It simply states (depicts graphically) that there are two theoretical extremes in the rate of taxation, both of which result in zero tax revenue. These are (obviously) 0 percent and 100 percent. At zero, the government clearly gets nothing, while at 100 percent it would get it all *once,* and that would be the end of it. There would be no means left with which to produce – not to mention *incentive* to do so.

The *Laffer Curve,* or theory, further – and *unarguably* – postulates that somewhere between the two extremes (0% and 100%) there is a rate that will result in the maximum tax revenue. That's it.

As pointed out earlier, during the Reagan years, the tax rates were reportedly cut in half, resulting in a doubling of the tax revenues. Certainly if one wishes to find the optimum tax rate, it should be a simple matter of lowering the rates until the revenues finally level off. However, when we have the *Fed* artificially adjusting the interest rates and the money supply (instead of having the market set the rates, and the money be backed by precious metal reserves) and the government regulating every other aspect of the economy, it is probably all but impossible to predict cause and effect with any accuracy.

So, if Laffer's prediction is correct, and an 11% tax across the board for personal incomes and net business sales – *"with no Laffer Curve at that"* – would equal all current federal tax revenues, a *lower tax rate* would result in *even greater revenues*, just as occurred under Reagan. I am therefore recommending an initial 10% - not on incomes, but on gross sales. Can anyone doubt that the effect on the overall economy would be dramatic? Is it not obvious that the resulting tax revenues would be proportionately large?

While no "progressive" would ever buy these arguments – even after they were (*as they already have been*) clearly demonstrated – my purpose here is *not to increase the tax revenues*. It is just the opposite. As the government is restricted to doing only those things specifically authorized by the *Constitution,* we will be able to simultaneously, cut the tax rates more over time.

I presume that this should take 5-10 years, by reducing spending by only 1% per year. If you weren't paying close attention, you would have missed the actual percentage. (At 1% per year off of the initial 10% rate, that would, in reality, represent a 10% cut in spending after the first year, 11.1%, after the second, 12.5% after the third, 14.3% after the fourth, and 16.7% after the fifth, totaling 64.6% at that rate in six years, and so forth, until 3 – 3 1/3% is achieved – taking the rate back to that of 2017. Now *that* is *real* reform!)

This, of course needs to occur at every level of government. Not only are the vast majority of states in huge financial difficulty, with crippling liabilities created by labor union pensions, but local governments across the country have also grown dramatically.

My ultimate recommended target is a 10% "Caesar's" Tax for all three levels of government – and I don't mean 10% each. I mean 10% total, or approximately 3 - 3 1/3 % for each of the three: Federal, State, and Local Governments.

Once again, can you imagine the prosperity and freedom that would ensue? Now, before you "come back down to earth," and say "this could never happen." I have one simple question: Who would prevent it? The liberal elites? No. They are a minority. The politicians? Absolutely not! They will now begin to work for us.

The bureaucrats? _ _ _ _ no! They only have jobs as long as we are willing to hire them – and we will no longer be willing to hire those whose services can be performed by the private sector. We have been paying their salaries, benefits, and retirement, all of which are on average twice that which we receive. Are *you* willing to continue that? Of course not, nor is anyone else who works! Why would we?

There is, of course, another group that might try to stop this – besides the media and Hollywood elites – and that is the large segment of the population that currently pays no taxes, but there are still more of those paying than those not.

Numerically speaking, of course, if we subtract the liberal elites from those of us who pay taxes, the number of those who do not is probably greater than those of us who would be in full support of this measure.

That does not take into account the fact that a larger than normal percentage of the demographic we are talking about (compared with higher income demographics) does not vote. We are also not taking into account that a large percentage of these people still share the traditional American values of hard work, independence, and opportunity; and that they will soon come to see that a renewed economic prosperity makes their lives far better than it currently is – in the oppressive state-controlled, excessively regulated economy.

We all, of course, remember the cry of *"No taxation without representation!"* Some will have heard by now the converse argument of *"No representation without taxation!"* There is a reason why there was initially a constitutional requirement to own property as a prerequisite to being able to vote. It was simply that without owning anything, a person had no stake in voting for the taxation or regulation of what was only owned by others.

I might, frankly, be willing for the lower income earners to opt out of paying taxes *along with relinquishing their right to vote* (their choice) *if* there were a way of accomplishing this without reinstituting the massive and intrusive bureaucracy (for verifying income status) which we would have just dismantled. Having said that, it seems right that each citizen should have both the responsibility of paying his or her way, and the privilege (and responsibility) of voting. (By way of comparison, rich and poor alike are expected to tithe under the Lord's plan. Are we wiser or more compassionate than *He?*)

Interestingly, between the sales tax being based on gross, and not net sales receipts, and all 12,000,000 (?) illegal immigrants paying their fair share, the tax revenues would unquestionably be in line with the reduced government bureaucracy that will result from balancing the budget.

I *might* also be willing for the sales tax to apply to *Internet* sales, if necessary – keeping in mind that the initial 10% would eventually be reduced to a third or more of that amount. There will be many who will argue that they do not want the government to have any access or control over the *Internet,* and, as I'm sure it's clear by now, I do not want the government to "control" *anything* for which it does not have clearly enumerated powers...but I *think* I'd rather have the government tax electronic Internet transactions than income....

This would also immediately resolve the issue of illegal immigrants not paying any federal taxes. They would now pay their full share along with everyone else.

This would also apply to every tourist or foreign visitor. Anyone living in the country for any length of time – and benefiting from the use of our (post-secondary) educational system, commerce, and other infrastructure would pay their fair share.

So, my friend, this is a matter for us to decide. It is no longer for the ruling class. We are once again the ruling class – and we outnumber the imposters.

3. Create a Constitutional Review Committee in both the House and the Senate, whose job it is to review each bill before it is allowed to go to the floor for debate, and require the authors of each bill to cite the specific Constitutional provisions upon which it is based.

In addition to citing *Constitution* and *Declaration* authority, the writers of each law would be required to defend both the purpose of the proposed law and the law itself, as it relates to the interpretive writings of the founders, recorded in original documents such as letters and other official records, and published works, such as *The Federalist Papers*.

References to case law would only be considered as a tertiary source, and where case law diverges from the writings of the founders, it will be considered of no legal weight. The practice of citing foreign case law would be strictly prohibited (with the exception of English Common Law, and other law traditions upon which the *Constitution* and *Declaration* were based) as modern foreign case law would have no relevance in determining the intent of the founders in writing the *Constitution* – which intent is, fortuitously, well documented.

4. **Enact mandatory term limits for all members of Congress.** This is perhaps the best example of how changes in society might well require amending our laws or constitutions as cited by Thomas Jefferson (and quoted earlier). It would appear that the founders did not anticipate the vast majority of our federally elected officials becoming 'career politicians.' I therefore recommend:

   Congressmen......2 Terms of 2 Years each.......Total: 4 Years
   Senators............2 Terms of 4 Years each.......Total: 8 Years

   Thus the average term would be 3-6 years or as many as 12 – *more than enough time* for a good (or bad) public servant!

5. **Repeal in its entirety the Federal Health Care Bill passed by the previous Congress, dissolving any and all agencies or boards set up thereunder.** De-fund any and all provisions thereof which are set to go into effect before the 2012 Presidential Election in the event that this proposed legislation is vetoed by the current President.

6. **Enact a Federal Statute *allowing* the sale of individual or family health insurance policies across state lines.** I find no authority in the *Constitution* for mandating that private or publicly-held businesses do this if they do not find it to be in their best interests, or that of their customers, but any federal restrictions thereon should be lifted.

7. **Institute Tort Reform** with specified limits of liability, or formulae for determining such limits for specified types of cases. Substantially stiffen the fines and other penalties for frivolous lawsuits, including, but not limited to, disbarment and paying plaintiffs' legal fees and all court costs. Require mandatory proof of ability to pay the above prior to initiating a suit.(Such laws should perhaps, be instituted by the states.)

8. **Repeal in its entirety the Financial Reform Bill passed by the previous Congress**, dissolving any and all agencies or boards set up thereunder.

De-fund any and all provisions thereof which are set to go into effect before the 2012 Presidential Election in the event that this proposed legislation is vetoed by the current President. De-fund the Financial Recovery Act - both acts having been passed against the expressed will of the voters. [*Note: The newly elected Republican-led Congress should move to repeal every bill passed during the "lame duck" session, for which the newly elected members did not vote.*]

9. **Divest the Federal Government of full or partial ownership in any and all formerly privately-held businesses**. This would, of course, include car companies, banks, and insurance companies. Dissolve the quasi-government agencies known as Fannie Mae and Freddy Mack, and immediately de-fund their continued operations.

10. **Immediately meet with the governors and sheriffs in states and towns along the Mexican border, to facilitate their efforts to police and protect their borders from illegal entry and other unlawful activities or threats.** Construct a continuous fence along the Mexican border, modeled on that employed by Israel along its border, and deploy Army or National Guard troops to assist the US Border Patrol and local and state law enforcement officials in the performance of their duties relative to protecting their borders. Dispatch the US Army to any occupied areas along the border that are deemed unsafe for US citizens. (Provide the necessary funds to perform these vital services by eliminating any federal agencies, such as the Department of Education, not specifically authorized by the *Constitution*, and not showing verifiable progress – such as a meaningful improvement in student test scores, in the case of the aforementioned Department – in the fulfillment of the recorded objectives for which it was originally instituted – provided that those objectives are found to be legal under the *Constitution*.)

11. **Conduct a full financial audit of the Federal Reserve,** and hold both Public and Congressional hearings on its purposes and procedures. Require that it cite both its *Constitution* and *Declaration* authorization for the Senate Constitutional Review Committee in the manner prescribed previously herein for any proposed legislation. If it should fail to satisfactorily meet the aforementioned requirements, it is to be abolished.

12. **Enact a Federal Marriage Amendment** for the purpose of defining and strengthening the Traditional Family as the universal building block of this or any other free society. If the nuclear family is not preserved, the nation cannot endure.

13. **Enact legislation to render null and void any programs or benefits to Congress – including, but not limited to retirement benefits or programs, health care, or any other legal immunities – not available to *any legal* citizen of the United States.**

14. **Provide greater legal remedies for judicial activism**, and hold both Public and Senate Hearings for the purpose of obtaining the input of both the Senate and US Citizens concerning remedies and penalties – such as impeachment and removal from the bench – of any Federal Judge who is found through a Senate Hearing to be guilty of legislating from the bench. Consider both making federal judges subject to election by the people, as well as the elimination of life-long appointments for Supreme Court Justices (both of which would require Constitutional Amendment). The practice of citing foreign case law would also be made illegal.

15. **Hold Public Hearings in the US Senate relative to our role and participation in both the United Nations, and the *IMF*** (International Monetary Fund), as well as the taxes and funding associated with our continued participation therein.

16. **Require that every proposed bill concern itself with a single issue.** Not only should earmarks be outlawed, but "riders" as well. They are there for one reason, and one reason alone, that being that they cannot stand (or pass) on their own merits. They should therefore be completely outlawed, and each congressman or senator be required to cast an up or down vote on the specific ("clean") piece of legislation being proposed. Period.

17. **Hold a Constitutional Convention** as provided in the *Constitution* for the purpose of amending the *Constitution* to include any and all of these provisions – when deemed necessary or preferable to the enactment of new statutes or legislation.

"Those who expect to reap the blessings of freedom, must, like men, undergo the fatigue of supporting it."

Thomas Paine

I will end by saying that while all of this will not be done overnight, it is within our power to do each of these things once we *decide* to do them. At this point in time, both our personal liberties and our economy have been decimated by the abandonment of both the principles and the legal framework and directives set forth in the *Constitution*.

Hear now the words of one of our greatest Presidents, and leaders, at whose feet the Rally of 8/28 was held some 6 1/2 weeks ago. He, like his peers among our Founders, seems to have seen down through the ages to the present day; thus his words are as applicable to us, here and now, as when they were spoken. I pray that we will heed them, and join him in pledging ourselves to the cause of rebuilding our nation, that it may once again become a "shining city on a hill."

Many of us were reserved to come forth in this day, and for this very purpose. I pledge to you that I will not be deterred from doing my part, and I am optimistic that together "with a firm reliance on ...divine Providence" we will succeed!

"Many free countries have lost their liberty, and ours may lose hers; but if she shall, be it my proudest plume, not that I was the last to desert, but that I never deserted her. I know that the great volcano at Washington, aroused and directed by the evil spirit that reigns there, is belching forth the lava of political corruption in a current broad and deep, which is sweeping with frightful velocity over the whole length and breadth of the land, bidding fair to leave unscathed no green spot or living thing; while on its bosom are riding, like demons on the waves of hell, the imps of that evil spirit, and fiendishly taunting all those who dare resist its destroying course with the hopelessness of their effort; and, knowing this, I cannot deny that all may be swept away. Broken by it I, too, may be; bow to it I never will."

President Abraham Lincoln – Speech, Springfield, Illinois, Dec 20, 1839. I, 137, in Archer H. Shaw, *The Lincoln Encyclopedia* (New York: Macmillan, 1950), p. 64. Full quote from *Project Gutenberg*.

"To sin by silence when they should protest makes cowards of men."

Abraham Lincoln

Final Note from the Author

The purpose of this book has been twofold:

1. I want those of us with the traditional American values of *individual liberty* (*personal freedom*, in a word), *limited (vastly smaller and less intrusive) government*, *lower taxes* (*now* literally half or more of our incomes), *hard work*, and *personal responsibility* (for our success or failure, our health care, every aspect of our lives that does not harm another) to understand that *WE* are both the mainstream and the majority of this country, and as such, *WE* will decide *how* – and *to what degree* – we will be taxed, regulated, and governed!

2. I want to *start the discussion* about what we must do *specifically* to restore our country to the roots of these very values. My list is not in any way the "Final Word," nor is it complete. (Most of my recommendations are, of course, simply a return to the *Constitution* and the Rule of Law!) As such, this list is simply a place to begin the dialogue and the debate...a *necessary* first step! So, please, *spread the word!*

As will be apparent to anyone who "did the math" while reading the "Cover Story," this book was written in a few short weeks, as a result of the challenge given by Glenn Beck at the 8/28 "Restoring Honor" rally in Washington, DC. There are, therefore, some recommendations in "The Call to Arms," which will require additional in-depth study and analysis. That, of course, will be done throughout the process in which they will be debated. In any case, the issues raised therein must be addressed as we embark upon the path of restoring our nation, and I stand by the principles upon which my recommendations are based. I will continue to address these and other critical issues, along with my proposed solutions, in regular postings on my blog and website:
www.UncommonSenseNow.com. I am also available to speak at Tea Party and 912 groups, churches, and other gatherings. To schedule a time, please contact me at:
Author@UncommonSenseNow.com.

Winning (in November 2010 and 2012) is only the beginning!

Appendix I

An Insightful Email Message

Some people have the ability to sum things up in such a way that they can be easily understood. This quote came from someone in the Czech Republic. Apparently a degree of geographic separation has enabled him to see clearly, and put things into perspective for those of us who may be too close to actually *see!*

"The danger to America is not Barack Obama but a citizenry capable of entrusting a man like him with the Presidency. It will be far easier to limit and undo the follies of an Obama presidency than to restore the necessary common sense and good judgment to a depraved electorate willing to have such a man for their president. The problem is much deeper and far more serious than Mr. Obama, who is a mere symptom of what ails America. Blaming the prince of the fools should not blind anyone to the vast confederacy of fools that made him their prince. The Republic can survive a Barack Obama, who is, after all, merely a fool. It is less likely to survive a multitude of fools such as those who made him their president."

Author's Comment:

This email was sent to me since I completed the book, but I felt it was relevant, as it points to *the source of* – and *the solution to* – *all* of our problems! We may with accuracy blame those who are, and have, for decades, been actively seeking to "fundamentally transform" this nation. The fact remains, however, that had we (as well as those who went before us), been doing our part, this could never have happened! It matters not, however, because we now have the opportunity, and the *privilege* to step forth and *save* both the *Constitution*, and the nation!

Whatever form of government we will have in the end will be exactly what we are willing to accept; no more, nor no less! We, THE PEOPLE, will have the ultimate say! The future of the nation is in our hands...as it has been all along!

"We the people are the rightful masters of both Congress and the courts, not to overthrow the Constitution but to overthrow the men who pervert the Constitution."   Abraham Lincoln

Appendix II

The following letter to the President from an "ordinary" citizen expresses clearly what the majority of Americans now think and feel about the "change" we were promised and have seen thrust upon us!

"WE NOTICED"

President Obama:

Today I read of your administrations' plan to re-define September 11 as a National Service Day. Sir, it's time we had a talk.

During your campaign, Americans watched as you made mockery of our tradition of standing and crossing your heart when the Pledge of Allegiance was spoken. You, out of four people on the stage, were the only one not honoring our tradition.
YES, "We noticed."

During one of your many speeches, Americans heard you say that you intended to visit all 57 states. We all know that Islam, not America has 57 states.
YES, "We noticed."

When President Bush leaned over at Ground Zero and gently placed a flower on the memorial, while you nonchalantly tossed your flower onto the pile without leaning over.
YES, "We noticed."

Every time you apologized to other countries for America's position on an issue we have wondered why you don't share our pride in this great country. When you have heard foreign leaders berate our country and our beliefs, you have not defended us. In fact, you insulted the British Crown beyond belief.
YES, "We noticed."

When your pastor of 20 years, "God-damned America" and said that 9/11 was "America's chickens coming home to roost" and you denied having heard recriminations of that nature, we wondered how that could be. You later disassociated yourself from that church and Pastor Wright because it was politically expedient to do so.
YES, "We noticed."

When you announced that you would transform America, we wondered why. With all her faults, America is the greatest country on earth. Sir, KEEP THIS IN MIND, "if not for America and the people who built her, you wouldn't be sitting in the White House now." Prior to your election to the highest office in this Country, you were a senator from Illinois and from what we can glean from the records available, not a very remarkable one.
YES, "We noticed."

All through your campaign and even now, you have surrounded yourself with individuals who are basically unqualified for the positions for which you appointed them. Worse than that, the majority of them are people who, like you, bear no special allegiance, respect, or affection for this country and her traditions.
YES, "We noticed."

You are 14 months into your term and every morning millions of Americans wake up to a new horror heaped on us by you. You seek to saddle working Americans with a health care/insurance reform package that, along with cap and trade, will bankrupt this nation.
YES, "We noticed."

We seek, by protesting, to let our representatives know that we are not in favor of these crippling expenditures and we are labeled "un-American", "racist", "mob". We wonder how we are supposed to let you know how frustrated we are. You have attempted to make our protests seem isolated and insignificant. Until your appointment, Americans had the right to speak out.
YES, "We noticed."

On September 11, 2001 there were no Republicans or Democrats, only Americans. And we all grieved together and helped each other in whatever way we could. The attack on 9/11 was carried out because we are Americans.
And YES, "We noticed."

There were many of us who prayed that as a black president you could help unite this nation. In six months you have done more to destroy this nation than the attack on 9/11. You have failed us.
YES, "We noticed."

September 11 is a day of remembrance for all Americans. You propose to make 9/11 a "National Service Day". While we know that you don't share our reverence for 9/11, we pray that history will report your proposal as what it is, a disgrace.
YES, "We noticed."

You have made a mockery of our *Constitution* and the office that you hold. You have embarrassed and slighted us in foreign visits and policy.
YES, "We noticed."

We have noticed all these things. We will deal with you. When Americans come together again, it will be to remove you from office. Take notice.

If you agree with this, please pass it on. If not, I'm sorry!

The originator of "We Noticed" is Faye Parrish of Bunnell, Florida, who told us she penned it in August 2009 and e-mailed it to several friends, after which it was posted on a number of blogs and published as a tribute to 9-11 on the FamilySecurityMatters.org website (http://www.snopes.com/politics/ soapbox/wenoticed.asp).

Author's Note:

This letter represents the views of millions of Americans who love their country, and share all of the traditional values of which I have spoken herein. It is to the author of this email, as well as the rest of the *true* mainstream, that I address myself. We (*you!*) are the one(s) who will once again make this country great…and remember, you (*we*) have just witnessed – brought about, actually! – what well may have been the biggest electoral victory in our nation's history!

Look at it as a bulletin (or *lightning bolt!*) *from Heaven*…to let us all know that with *God on our side*, or, more accurately, *with us on God's side* – the side of *personal* freedom, *personal* charity, and *personal* accountability – we can and will succeed in restoring our nation as a beacon of freedom, prosperity, goodness, Godliness, and hope for all of mankind!

In fact, not only is it "possible"...with His help, as we each do our part, we will become unstoppable! (As George Soros recently admitted, *even he* can't stop it! For more on him, visit: http://www.freerepublic.com/focus/f-news/1173853/posts.)

Yes, my friends, if we will each do our part*, we can and will win!* In fact, I believe there are enough of us who have already begun to speak out and become involved, that "we have *already* won!" – as Glenn Beck stated at his rally on 8/28.

The question for each of us individually is simply this:

Will I be able to look myself, my children, my grandchildren, and my God in the eye...and say, "I did my part!"?

I have faith that you *can,* and *will* do it. We *all can!* So *let's get started!* We can all use the *Internet* now to let those that we care about know where we stand. That is perhaps the most important thing that any of us can do...so spread the word! Start *today!* Start right now! Send a brief email to everyone on your list, and let them know how important that you feel the time between now and the coming (2012) election is! (If you haven't put together an email list, do it now! If you don't know how, ask anyone who uses email regularly, and they will be happy to show you!) This *one simple process* is changing – *and has already changed* – our country *for the better!*

These may seem like small steps, but the ocean itself is made of nothing but countless small drops of water. Don't worry whether anyone else follows your lead. Many will, and you should *ask your family and friends* to get involved by simply *passing things along*, but the thing that matters most to each of us individually is that we do the right thing *ourselves;* and we don't have to quit our 'day jobs' in order to do it!

We just have to take these simple steps, along with *becoming informed,* and not being afraid to *let others know where we stand,* as we associate with people in the normal *day to day* of our lives – and the best place to *start* becoming informed is on *Fox News,* especially with *Glenn Beck.* You can *start* being a force for good *today* by telling those you meet to watch as well! (Most of you already are watching, but many of your friends and family *aren't...yet!*)

You, and those who come after you, will be grateful...and *happy* that you did these few simple things...and if you want to become more involved once you have done these few things, that option will also be open to you.

God bless us that we may each do our part!

The Author – T. M. Ballantyne, Jr.

Please email me with your comments, questions, and thoughts at: **Author@UncommonSenseNow.com**

Thanks for all that you *have* done...and all that you *will* do... **beginning now!**

www.UncommonSenseNow.com

About the Author

("All You Need to Know!")

This was the title of a previous chapter, in case you've forgotten!

I was born, and subsequently raised, in Houston (Bellaire), Texas, in 1950. I have a sister and two brothers. My brothers are conservative, for the most part; my sister lived with her husband and three children 'inside the Beltway' for most of her adult life....

My wife, Jan, and I met at the University of Texas, and were married in Logan, UT. We have since become the parents of eight wonderful children, all born in Houston. We relocated to Arizona in 2003, where we now live, near our children and grandchildren.

Some 25-30 years ago we moved to Nashville, TN, where we raised our children. It was there that I had my first taste of citizen involvement. I became a regular caller on the Phil Valentine radio talk-show. My 'handle' was "Tom from Brentwood" (There were a few imposters!)

Towards the end of our time in *Music City*, I became involved in what became known as the *"Tennessee Tax Revolt."* It was the "original" Tea Party – of *modern* times, at least. We would gather with our signs and placards at *Legislative Plaza*, at the foot of the state capitol, and thousands of people would drive by and honk in opposition to the income tax. Not only did they honk, but they would drive around the plaza over and over again, honking as they went. The noise was deafening, and the excitement, contagious...and we defeated the income tax! *To this day, some 9-10 years later, Tennessee is one of only a handful of states that still do not have an income tax!*

I attempted to write a book about the experience, but eventually ran out of money (I had a family to support!), and put the manuscript aside. Nevertheless, I learned much through the process and have written several books since then. It is my intention that this one will play a role in influencing the good people of this country to step forward and reinstate their authority! We are in a battle for the soul of our nation, and we intend to win! I ask only that we each do what we individually know to be right! As we do that, and let our family and friends know clearly where we stand, *we will succeed!*

The Author – Palm Desert, CA. 2008

www.ingramcontent.com/pod-product-compliance
Lightning Source LLC
LaVergne TN
LVHW051839080426
835512LV00018B/2964